MEGA MEDIA

How Market Forces Are Transforming News

NANCY MAYNARD

MEGA MEDIA

How Market Forces Are Transforming News

By Nancy Hicks Maynard

© 2000 Maynard Partners Incorporated
2109 Broadway
New York, NY 10023

(212) 721-1710
Fax (212) 579-2633
www.nancymaynard.com

Cover photo © Fukuhara, Inc./CORBIS

Library of Congress Cataloging in Publication data:

Maynard, Nancy Hicks.
Mega Media: How Market Forces Are Transforming News /
Maynard, Nancy Hicks.

176 p.; 29 cm.

1. Mass media—Economic aspects. 2. Mass media—Economic
aspects—United States. 3. Mass media—Ownership.
4. Mass media and technology. 5. Mass media—United States.

I. Title
P96 .E25 M385 2000
ISBN 0-9701292-0-3   00-500009

TRAFFORD

This book was published on-demand in cooperation with Trafford Publishing.

Suite 6E, 2333 Government St., Victoria, B.C. V8T 4P4, CANADA
Phone   250-383-6864   Toll-free 1-888-232-4444 (Canada & US)
Fax   250-383-6804   E-mail   sales@trafford.com
Web site www.trafford.com trafford publishing is a division of trafford holdings ltd.
Trafford Catalogue #00-0083   www.trafford.com/robots/00-0083.html

10   9   8   7   6   5   4

Table of Contents

Acknowledgements

This report was made possible by the generous support of The Freedom Forum. I am especially grateful to Chairman and Chief Executive Officer Charles L. Overby for approving the project and encouraging its completion. Also, Adam Clayton Powell III provided help with technology issues and by making available his extensive network of experts. And Newseum Historian Eric Newton played a key role, providing context for the story of news and invaluable advice along the way.

The Rockefeller Foundation also supported this work.

At many points, I had the assistance of several brilliant business strategists. They include Katherine Fulton of Global Business Network; Kathy Lynn-Cullotta of Lynn-Cullotta Consulting; and David L. Sibbet of Grove Consultants International. Also, economists Roger G. Noll of Stanford University and Hal R. Varian, chairman of U.C. Berkeley's School of Information, helped frame the issues.

In digging for facts and figures I was assisted by Lisa Donneson, Helen C. Poot, Antonious L. K. Porch and Thomas G. Davidson.

My able assistants Cindy Liu, Alicia Carmona and Nina Spensley managed the logistics of field work and manuscript production with great skill and humor.

Maurice R. Fliess of The Freedom Forum and Mary A. Anderson edited the manuscript with a sharp eye and cursor. Their drive for clarity dramatically improved the report.

The inspiration for this study came in large measure from James N. Rosse, former provost of Stanford University and recently retired CEO of Freedom Communications Inc. He was the most faithful advocate of this research. There is no way to thank him enough for his contribution.

Introduction

Why this report?

The 21st century is here. Promise and predictions abound. One of the fiercest debates examines the future of news. Media observers worry that news is becoming so frivolous and profit-driven that it will become useless as an instrument of public understanding.

Strangely, little helpful information has emerged from debates over the future of information. The main reason: The United States has a news industry and a news-criticism industry. The industry is reinventing itself around seismic changes in information technology. Some of the new journalism falls short by almost any standard. The critics are mostly reporters, editors or producers who mourn the good old days. They often scold but rarely prescribe solutions.

Sadly, journalists who chronicle and interpret social change become offended when the same trends transform their own newsrooms. These gatekeepers of civic literacy have become, instead, gatekeepers of generation-based traditions, unable to adapt their professional principles to changing times. They follow a well-worn path of protectors of the intellectual status quo. The same mindset, centuries ago, opposed the printing press, fearing it would promote ignorance by discouraging memorization.

This report attempts to find an honest and different way to understand the future of news across media. Its assessment begins in the marketplace and follows a maze of business practices back to the newsroom — not to celebrate the economic trends driving the news but to identify the true leverage points shaping this brave new digital-information world.

This approach to news analysis is akin to assessing a meal's nutritional value. No longer is the news a traditional fixed menu. Today's 24-hour news cycle offers a burgeoning buffet from newspapers, magazines, television, cable, radio and the Internet. Its nutrient value depends on which brain food we order. All desserts? Clearly not. The issue becomes whether the kitchen offers enough healthy options, not the amount of "junk" in the mix.

This report is the result of almost three years of meetings, interviews and research, beginning at The Freedom Forum Media Studies Center in New York City. As chair of the center from 1996 to 1997, I began a series of focused conversations among journalists, theorists, executives and economists.

All of us tried to imagine the quality of news the public might demand into the future. More often than not, the journalists would set out wish lists of how news should evolve, and the economists would explain why those views might be fanciful. Robust enterprise reporting led the list of difficult choices.

As we started our study, a pall hung over journalism. News-media fortunes had slumped. Newsprint prices hit all-time highs. Advertising spending flattened. TV networks and newspapers trimmed reporting staffs. Consolidation loomed. Sensationalism threatened to overwhelm watchdog journalism. The Internet marched on. Bill Gates of Microsoft Corp. seemed poised to swallow big pieces of the news business, especially profitable classified ads.

By 1997, media markets roared back. Journalists were relieved. But the basic questions about how news might evolve would not, could not, go away.

···

MEDIA USAGE (hours per person per year)

Medium	1985	1990	1995	1997	2000 (projected)
Television	1505	1470	1575	1610	1555
Broadcast	1320	1120	1019	1023	854
Network stats.	985	780	836	810	666
Independent stats.	335	340	183	213	188
Cable	185	350	556	581	701
Basic	100	260	468	491	592
Premium	85	90	88	90	109
VCR	15	30	45	55	58
Movies in theaters	12	12	12	12	12
Radio	—	1135	1091	1067	1074
Reading	375	360	348	347	331
Newspapers	185	175	165	161	154
Books	80	95	99	104	98
Magazines	110	90	84	82	79
Computers	—	13	33	53	74
Online/Internet	—	1	7	22	37
Home video games	—	12	24	29	35
Educational software	—	<1	2	2	2

Source: Veronis, Suhler and Associates as quoted from U.S. Census

This approach to news analysis is akin to assessing a meal's nutritional value. No longer is the news a traditional fixed menu. Today's 24-hour news cycle offers a burgeoning buffet.

So the study continued, with more than 200 interviews of news executives, other journalists, academics, media moguls, bankers, regulators — a dizzying cast of characters.

In addition, the study reviewed national trends over time concerning reporting styles, major events, and changes in media technology or ownership. We also rearranged the statistical measurements of news-media financial trends to better understand the last 50 years. To keep the subject matter manageable, the report includes newspapers, broadcast and cable television, and the Internet. It does not analyze radio or newsmagazines. And its subject matter is domestic, not international, although broader global lessons can be drawn from its results.

Actually, this study was born when I was a student at Stanford Law School 15 years ago. I looked at the Federal Communications Commission's moves to deregulate television, introducing that medium to industrial ownership.

After decades of public hostility to this idea, the new FCC rules allowed General Electric to purchase RCA, parent of the NBC television network. A media buying spree ensued.

My interest in media ownership was not coincidental. I undertook the Stanford study several years after my late husband, Robert C. Maynard, and I purchased *The Oakland Tribune,* a troubled California daily we owned for a decade.

When we bought the *Tribune,* media commentators told us we could not survive as an independent, unionized, undercapitalized venture in one of America's most competitive media markets. To them, the fact that we were also the first and only African-American family — unwealthy at that — to own and run a general-circulation daily made our prospects that much worse.

As it turned out, the naysayers were right about the difficulty. (We finally sold the newspaper in 1992 to a local competitor, who merged it with four existing dailies, creating an efficiency and profitability we could not achieve.)

MEDIA CANNIBALIZATION

Internet users consume:

More	Less
• cable news	• TV movies
• news magazines	• TV talk shows
• business newspapers	• daily newspapers
• specialty magazines	• family magazines
• science	
• computer	

    • Than non-Internet users.
    • Variance intensifies with time.

Source: Forrester Research

....

But they were wrong about the possibilities. They underestimated the residual strength of even a crippled media franchise.

From our perspective, the issues we confronted at the *Tribune* were knottier and subtler than the often-blunt media critics comprehended. And they resonate still in today's heated debates. Should the news business:

• Invest capital first in news content or in technology and distribution?
• Diversify across media or go deeply into one?
• Focus on discrete geographic markets or spread out and compete?

The answers are rarely either/or, but the players' varied emphases will affect financial indicators — and news.

This report differs from most others because I've filtered the research through many experiences in more than 30 years in the news business — in the newsroom (mostly *The New York Times*), in the owner's suite (*The Oakland Tribune*) and in the boardroom (Tribune Co. of Chicago and the Public Broadcasting Service). Also influencing the analysis are my consulting engagements for telephone companies, some of which wanted to develop business partnerships with newspapers.

From this filtered view has come, I hope, a broad look at why journalism is the way it is and how it is changing (or could change) to better serve the public interest. While not minimizing the real threats to civic education should news deteriorate, this report shows how technology, market forces and changing lifestyles are creating new distribution systems for news.

At the same time, this report is no techno-celebration of computerized news. Instead, it explores the complexity of change, the promise of technol-

> **News-media leaders can either avoid or manage many perils with foresight, sufficient capital and a willingness to embrace a new world. Companies can invest and merge, changing their fortunes in the process. In short, the wolf by the door doesn't always enter.**

ogy and the possibly meaningful improvements in substance.

There will always be news, if only to fulfill our curiosity about our neighbors. We humans are a social species, after all — and, I might add, a storytelling one. News fills that need. Trends in technology and distribution, too real to ignore, pose both threats and opportunities. But journalists can survive change with their integrity intact.

Unpredictability also figures into the mix. Business conditions change all the time. Opportunities as well as threats show up. Sometimes, conventional wisdom is wrong. Events, invention, regulation and a host of trends drive the news industries in often-unexpected ways.

Under media consolidation the much-vaunted, or maligned, attempts at synergy are not always as efficient as planned. News-media leaders can either avoid or manage many perils with foresight, sufficient capital and a willingness to embrace a new world. Companies can invest and merge, changing their fortunes in the process. In short, the wolf by the door doesn't always enter. That was a lesson from Oakland and one that loomed large in reviewing media-company strategies for this study.

Developing successful models for the future of news is complex but not rocket science. The fundamentals still apply. As in the past, success will grow from a mixture of superior market position, superb marketing practices and inventive content, including great journalism — all married to the right technology and distribution systems. As always, boldness can be bankable. And leadership, creativity and integrity are bankable.

The current profit fixation usually does not drive substantive change. A business plan in search of an idea rarely succeeds. Rather, innovation in search of capital has a better track record in all industries, including the news.

One need only remember the origins of Cable News Network, America Online and *USA TODAY*. Together, they are arguably the most influential news innovations of the last two decades. Each was ridiculed when launched: CNN was the Chicken Noodle Network, not a grown-up network-news organization. AOL would never beat the early online powerhouses, Prodigy and CompuServe, right? People called *USA TODAY* "McPaper" because it served up bite-size portions of news. The business world considered all of them to be financially perilous, their paths to profit long and tortured.

But Ted Turner, who founded CNN, had an idea to validate Marshall McLuhan's theory that the mass media, especially television, were creating a global village.

AOL's Steve Case and his digital frontiersmen resisted a safe rescue by Microsoft. They had their own vision of an Internet community, and 21 million subscribers have joined it.

The same was true for Al Neuharth's push to publish *USA TODAY*. I asked recently how he knew a new national daily would become America's most successful newspaper launch in more than 50 years — now the country's largest daily, with more than 2 million individual and bulk sales.

"I didn't," he replied. "I had a hunch."

He went for it based on Gannett Co.'s history with *FLORIDA TODAY* on the Space Coast, plus the company's acquisition experience.

"Besides," he added, "the idea of simply continuing to acquire and manage more newspapers was boring."

In retrospect, *USA TODAY* wasn't a bad bet.

CNN Chairman W. Thomas Johnson recently summed up the challenge facing him and his industry compatriots: "You can't predict the future of news. You have to invent it."

And so he is inventing it, along with thousands of other editors and executives who care deeply about news and who find its transformation-in-progress at least as exciting as it may be vexing.

Together, they are remaking the personality and processes of the news, shedding its 20th century industrial manners for something more appropriate to our new millennium. It's a bit of an uncharted journey, but no one serious about success, financial or journalistic, can afford to sit out the ride.

Forces Driving the Future of News

The Internet. High-definition television. Electronic marketing and sales. All promise to change news as we've known it. This study has identified seven driving forces whose courses will have the greatest impact:

1. Digitization: Eating the News

Digital information technology will affect news more than previously imagined — much the way refrigeration changed everything about food production and consumption. It threatens the very definition of news as we've known it. It changes the rhythm of news consumption, while the tempo of news production remains fairly rigid, Web sites notwithstanding.

2. Distribution: Give Us Your Eyeballs, Your Ears

There is no content without distribution.

In the chicken-and-egg riddle of which comes first — content or distribution — distribution is ascendant as companies try to rebuild mass audiences for news, information and entertainment. Media are focused on growing audience share — at the expense of content, including the news.

Only with completion of consolidation, currently under way, will media strike a new balance, cut the cost of providing information to individual consumers and determine which advertising markets to sell to.

3. Market Brand: What's in a Name?

As media companies work hard to maintain a market of consumers who indirectly pay for the news, a host of readership, viewership and technological issues have engaged them. The old mission was clear, but the new imperatives are not.

Collaborative filtering, duopoly, zoning, affinity purchasing and other marketing devices provide tools that are useful to gain advertisers yet complex for media companies unaccustomed to the number of steps required to piece together an audience today. More basically, they seek to define themselves anew.

They ask: Who are we now? What are the elements of success? How do we sell it? Where is the news in it all?

4. Generation Gap: The Soft Underbelly of Change

Generational clash is the soft underbelly of gonzo planning in news-media companies. Baby boomers have captured the newsrooms of traditional media, especially print media.

These newsroom leaders disdain the learning styles and information-getting habits of younger people. They lack appreciation for a future, growing audience. Their attitudes could impede appropriate investments in news, programs and marketing for the next generation of citizens — and leaders.

5. Localism: Why the Internet and Bill Gates Can't Kill the Local Media Market

Despite predictions that the Internet undermines a geographic sense of community — and it does to some extent — commerce is local and will mostly remain so. With a few national exceptions, the news-media marketplace will be mostly local as well.

Three years ago, the focus of every news-media business plan was to beat back Bill Gates and Microsoft Corp. from overtaking local news companies with Web sites and information. Gates didn't succeed but not for lack of trying. It was just too expensive to grow commerce deeply into local markets from a national platform. In the information world, local still rules.

That doesn't mean Microsoft is no longer a threat. Its automobile and real-estate Web sites skim off advertising from newspapers. And today's Internet model is anything but local. National and multinational portals with their economies of scale have amassed great marketplace power.

This dynamic mimics the dawn of television, when networks and their big audiences initially dominated for economic reasons. Over the decades, power shifted to local affiliates and stayed there, especially in news programming.

Historically, business success comes to companies whose plans are not easy to replicate. Competitors can easily match pricing; they cannot easily match intrinsically local information or service. Without local partners, at least, few national entities could afford to be simultaneously global and local. The question today: Who will those partners be?

6. Federal Policy: The Wild Card

Our free press is covered with federal fingerprints.

Federal policies and rules determine much about news-media health. In fact, a regulatory decision to allow pharmaceutical companies to advertise prescription drugs on television is partially what built the surge in advertising revenue during the course of this study.

Other rules still under consideration could help keep news organizations financially healthy into the future. Government's policy-steering role, a hidden hand, wields great power.

Much of the current consolidation resulted from the Federal Communications Commission's rule allowing cable and telephone companies to merge — to increase competition for local phone services.

More recent changes in television-ownership rules — allowing multiple channel ownership in a single market — produced more consolidation. A similar rule change for radio a few years ago has allowed some companies to own 700 or 800 radio stations apiece, as many as eight in the same market.

Cross-ownership rules prohibiting newspaper ownership of broadcast entities in their markets is the next big puzzle piece on the FCC's rule-making plate. Newspaper-industry representatives have petitioned the FCC to waive this restriction and support measures before Congress to repeal the ban. And Tribune Co.'s announced intention to acquire Times Mirror is a direct challenge to the rule.

7. Advertising: "Funny Money" and Other Issues

While still central to news-media revenue, advertising will be only one part of an increasingly complex revenue stream. The following issues will largely determine the shape of things to come:

• The shrinking mass audiences of traditional media are still bigger than any others in the fractured media market and command more value to advertisers, in some cases. How long will this continue?

• The new "clustering" technologies to identify potential online customers are not as powerful as previously believed and may not provide the online revenue boost they promise. Highly touted "collaborative filtering" software at best just confirms obvious behaviors, experts report. Also, the risk of privacy infractions makes Webmeisters cautious about using the new capabilities at all. Some Web sites strive for a "low creepy factor" in targeted advertising — "creepy" meaning intrusiveness, however users perceive it.

• On news Web sites, real-estate brokerages, financial services, job fairs and auto auctions are part of the new classified advertising. Another part is the system of sales-commission arrangements between advertisers and media.

• Accounting practices for these new revenue sources will determine how much money is available for news. If Internet businesses book the revenue as their own, who pays for the news?

So, the news business today is like the Wild West, in digital drag. Many rules are yet to be written, and the builders of the new order aren't shy about making them.

One of the boldest of the new media cowboys is Mel Karmazin, CEO of CBS, soon to be merged with Viacom. He's created a new currency — call it virtual equity — by trading advertising time on CBS television and radio networks for equity stakes in dot-com companies. His reasoning: Many of these companies spend most of their capital from going public on marketing to grow the company. Bartering would be a more efficient use of resources. Other companies are following suit.

Consumers are equally bold in making the rules, and finding the sweet spot of commerce is daunting. People expect Internet information and some services to be free. Broadband companies sometimes give away computers to ensure a steady customer base for up to three years.

Most news and information providers expect to ride out the changes the traditional way — charging advertisers and targeting messages to individual users, based on digital marketing's promise using Internet-browser technology. Adapting old ways to new realities while developing new Internet product lines is one business model for news companies.

In short, the news-media marketplace is a rough and complicated environment these days. Bigger entities can manage the complexity more easily, but for them, news is a smaller piece of the whole.

Ultimately, news providers must think in multiple dimensions and weigh their priorities as never before, choosing whether to emphasize distribution or content; bigness or smallness; local depth or national breadth; core medium or convergence; and passive or interactive marketplaces.

CHAPTER 1

Digitization: Eating the News

Imagine this: Three months ago, your local newspaper or TV station carried a story about the rampant infection rate at a hospital in town. You missed it, although you remember friends discussing it. Today, your doctor scheduled you for surgery at that very hospital. Suddenly, you need to know what that story said. How do you find it?

Not many years ago, you would have called the newspaper to try to identify the date of the article and purchase a back copy. Or you might have tried the local library. It would have been a hit-or-miss process, time-consuming at best.

If the story had run on television, finding it would have taken more effort and money and would have been more difficult, if not impossible. Local TV stations simply don't have back-issue departments.

In short, you had no guarantee of catching up with the news when you wanted it. Information supply and demand could be radically out of sync. The day after publication, facts became scarce. Companies such as LEXIS-NEXIS and Information on Demand charged hundreds or thousands of dollars to route the right facts to the right place at the right time. Keeping up with trends was difficult except for those with great interest or resources.

Today, you'd simply sign on to the newspaper's or station's Web site and search an archive. At a few station Web sites, you could download and watch the story. On the newspaper site, you might pay a fee for an old article, but you'd gladly do so. The information, worthless to you when the newspaper ran it, is valuable now.

The role of computers and the Internet in today's information revolution has widespread — and some not so obvious — implications for news gathering and consumption.

Note: Certain terms in this report are defined in a Glossary found on page 174.

Effect No. 1: Digitization preserves news like refrigeration preserves food

Before the World Wide Web came into general use around 1995, people consumed news much as they did food in pre-refrigeration days. Families bought what was fresh because they had limited ability to preserve it. Buy and eat fresh fish on Friday, or lose it.

The news business ran the same way. Stories might not have been vital to most people on a given day, but unless consumed or saved when presented, only scholars or commercial interests willing to pay search firms large sums could retrieve them.

The 20th century began with almost daily food shopping for city folk. The 21st century and the new millennium begin with mostly weekly shopping trips that haul in large amounts of food — some consumed immediately, most refrigerated or frozen. Families use items in cold storage when and how they decide to consume them. Occasional needs for a quart of milk or specialty items merit quick, supplemental shopping trips.

The digitization of news, then, is like food refrigeration: All presumptions about freshness, perishability, production, delivery times and methods are in the consumer's favor. Search engines "defrost" information when we want it. The public largely controls what it knows and when it knows it.

News has never been just what newspapers publish or broadcasters air. In the broadest sense, it is anything people don't know. The digital revolution amplifies this effect. We pay attention to a few major events or disasters, other matters we want to know about in the moment, plus more topics we stumble across along the way.

That's a simple proposition on its face but one with potentially seismic consequences for news as we know it. It promises to change everything about the way journalists identify, organize, package and produce the news, 24-hour news cycles notwithstanding.

A morning newspaper when no one is home to read it? Evening television news while the family is working or otherwise engaged? An advertising base tied to these changing habits and pleased to pay higher prices for whatever audience is left? Breaking news covered extensively on television, cable or the Internet, hours before a newspaper goes to press? A running story obsessing the public?

Back to food. Digitization creates more "frozen-food news" that's easy to use. It changes how companies distribute and sell news and how often we buy it with our attention or dollars. It will never wholly replace the present patterns of news consumption. But to the degree it changes those historic patterns, it will change the economics of the news industry.

Effect No. 2: Digital information technology shifts time valuation away from the classic economic model

Because news industries are mostly advertising-supported, economists have traditionally calculated the value of news media in two ways: the number of people reading or watching, and the time they spend with the product. They consider consumer time to be a proxy for payment for television news and entertainment — and for newspapers as well, since publication subscription prices are relatively modest. Cable's hefty pricing structure challenges those assumptions.

The traditional calculus has moved into cyberspace as well, where Web publishers sometimes count page views more seriously than the number of site visitors. Because consumers bore into a site one screen at a time, page views help quantify how interested each visitor is in the site and, therefore, how much time she spends there.

For most of the 20th century, with its global wars and major geopolitical conflict, news was perishable. It had to be consumed when published or aired because each day's events superseded the last. Today's news was currency. Yesterday's was fish wrap. Who cared about it tomorrow?

During the second half of the century, the speed and complexity of modern life increased demand for trend stories and investigations. The perishability and value of day-to-day news changed in the public mind. It isn't as important to know each little development as it is to know as soon as possible the events that advance a story.

Digital information retrieval is changing this time-value equation. With few exceptions, today's news is free, but you may pay to get yesterday's. Breaking-news coverage is free, but you might pay to search for meaningful news, such as that story on hospital infection.

Generally, companies that tried to get Internet users to pay for general, day-to-day information have failed. Those include business sites, such as the Cowles information Web site, Simba. Also, Microsoft's Slate magazine took more than 100,000 unpaid subscribers down to 20,000 paid subscribers before it reverted to free access. Even though Dow Jones & Co. successfully signed up some 300,000 paid subscribers to its Wall Street Journal Interactive edition, it has added less comprehensive, free services.

In this environment, information is a commodity. Its value comes from added insights, services or consumer time. Even tech guru Esther Dyson often said she wanted to offer the proprietary newsletter that launched her business, Release 1.0, for free, then make money from consultant engagements generated by the publication. Her publisher/partner wouldn't allow it.

Lore has developed that information should be "free" on the Web. In the Internet's early days, futurist Stewart Brand was often quoted as saying,

**Especially now, the Internet means "free."
The business model: Hook the consumer. Create a
relationship. Demonstrate value. Wait for commerce
to flow. Capture consumer value in attention,
purchases or transaction fees.**

"Information wants to be free." He was speaking more to free expression than free pricing. Over time, though, and especially now, the Internet means "free." The business model: Hook the consumer. Create a relationship. Demonstrate value. Wait for commerce to flow. Capture consumer value in attention, purchases or transaction fees.

Digital technology, then, allows the public to align its need to know with everything that's available. And it allows information purveyors to price for value all but today's commodity news.

The public's changing valuation of news in a digital world shows up in Net surfers' media-consumption patterns — pitted against the value of traditional editors' information "meal," served hot in a newspaper, magazine or TV program for consumption before going stale.

Internet users consume more cable news, more newsmagazines and more business newspapers than their offline counterparts, who view more television and read more daily newspapers. The differences are sometimes small but intensify the longer a person uses the Internet, according to Forrester Research. Its survey showed that Internet users consume:

- More cable news, focusing on breaking stories.
- Fewer daily newspapers with their eclectic mix of breaking news, trend articles, investigative pieces and lifestyle stories.
- More newsmagazines, which summarize and interpret last week's news.
- More business newspapers and science or computer magazines.

This suggests that attitudes are changing from "I must get the news right now" to "The news is there when I'm ready, and I'll pay for what I want or need."

Other studies underscore the Internet's influence. Roper Starch Worldwide found, for example, that 91% of Internet users conduct research online, 87% e-mail families and friends, and 73% get news. Chat rooms, e-commerce and portfolio management were found to be much less popular activities. Similar studies by Jupiter Communications listed e-mail as the No. 1 online activity, followed by news and research.

Clearly, new patterns are emerging. How news providers organize resources and coverage around these patterns will determine much about the future of news.

That may speak to Sam Donaldson's move from the ABC White House beat and its newsmagazine "Prime Time Live" and onto the Internet as ABC's big name on the Web.

Effect No. 3: Digitization reduces news production costs

Neil W. Patterson, senior vice president of finance and operations for ABC News, likes to compare digital news gathering with the traditional methods. Not so long ago, covering a major news event required 13 cases of equipment and a field production staff. Now a few cameras, a briefcase-size editing device and a satellite link are all that's needed for most stories.

"The savings on excess baggage fees alone is huge," Patterson said. Additional savings in transmission costs and staff reductions cut about 10%, which was plowed back into coverage, he said. Those are but a few tools for managing the network's 1,300 staff members worldwide, whose costs had increased 3% to 4% a year through 1998.

ABC has also experimented with virtual studios, a generational advance in the "blue screen" technology that weather reporters commonly use. A virtual studio is a computer-generated set image, projected onto a plain blue backdrop.

Sets and their engineering needs make up 20% of ABC's news budget, and the virtual studio can cut those cost substantially, Patterson said.

"It's a 6,000-square-foot studio vs. an office, a blue screen and one-third the staffing," he said. "It looks fabulous."

ABC's incremental savings show the growing impact of digital technology on news production. Throughout the world, production systems built around digital servers are adding flexibility and efficiency while often reducing costs.

One early user of the technology was Bloomberg L.P., the financial services information giant. Long before general news organizations employed such platforms, Bloomberg equipped its staff with workstations that allowed them to input stories once and easily edit them in text or broadcast form.

CNN's early success was its ability to build a franchise around digital technology. Compared with the established networks' budgets, CNN dramatically slashed news-operation costs. Its production efficiency allows it to quickly and easily repackage its stories for all of its news, financial, sports or international channels at low additional costs.

Computer-assisted reporting hasn't replaced shoe leather or the telephone, but it has helped news organizations to crunch large amounts of data and discern patterns that were previously invisible.

NBC and its cable-news progeny, MSNBC and CNBC, have the same technological advantages, which is one reason why NBC News is profitable while other network news organizations are not.

The network manages production systems through central facilities, with all information available to all programs all the time: Cable operations and servers reside in Manhattan and Secaucus, N.J.; affiliate productions operate in Charlotte, N.C.; and the Web site publishes from Microsoft Corp. in Redmond, Wash. All operations can interact and share information instantaneously through NBC's digital management system. Editorial protocols include checks and balances on use of information — for example, MSNBC.com must consult with network news executives in New York before promoting segments from "Dateline NBC."

In fairness, more than technology differentiates NBC from its broadcast competitors. NBC saw itself as a single news operation and invested in equipment to support that view.

Other news networks' programs operated as individual, competitive fiefdoms. Until last season, for example, ABC staffed each news program separately, sharing no resources among "Prime Time Live," "20/20," "World News Tonight," "Good Morning America," "Nightline" and "This Week." That has changed. Today, its new state-of-the-art studio in Times Square, built for GMA, is becoming a hub for an increasing number of programs, including its 24-hour millennium coverage marathon.

At the local and regional level, all-news cable channels have sprouted in 34 metropolitan areas, according to the Radio and Television News Directors Foundation. They use a digital camera and a single reporter/camera operator to transmit a story directly to headquarters for necessary packaging for its newscast.

In print, and now in broadcast as well, The Associated Press has used digital technology to lower the cost of news gathering. Its electronic darkroom, for instance, eliminated film-processing costs for newspapers that gave up traditional photo processing.

A.H. Belo Corp. and Tribune Co. both use digital platforms to connect newspaper coverage, multimedia Washington bureaus, Internet offerings, cable and broadcast news stations: Belo in Texas and the Pacific Northwest, Tribune in Chicago and Florida.

USA TODAY built its national franchise with satellite transmissions to regional printing sites around the country, a similar digital infrastructure to those of *The Wall Street Journal* and the national editions of *The New York Times.*

Local newspapers investing heavily in digital information management include *The Arizona Republic* in Phoenix.

"We've taken the time, money and effort to get the technology right," says Louis A. (Chip) Weil, CEO of Central Newspapers Inc., which owns the *Republic.* "We employed a theory [called] 'pillars of information,' in which we capture information once and publish it as many times and in as many forms as you would like."

The technology project, which cost more than $32 million, included fiber-optic wiring of the *Republic*'s new 10-story downtown building. It is expanding to CNI's *Indianapolis Star* as well.

An early success of the new system has been the expansion of local news and advertising zoning, *Republic* Publisher John Oppedahl said. Last year, for example, the newspaper created four new zones in a targeted growth area, six days a week, publishing an additional 160 pages each week with no additional design or printing staff, he said.

Effect No. 4: Digitization improves reporting

Digital information technology doesn't just make news cheaper, it makes news better.

Run down the list of recent journalism prize winners. Except for features, arts coverage or breaking news, most of the stories are data-driven investigative pieces made possible by digital information technology.

Some past winning topics: Improper gun use by police in Washington, D.C. Chemical sterilization exported to Third World countries. Key technologies exported to China. French fries exported to Japan (as a window on the Asian financial crisis). All used databases to get or manage information.

Computer-assisted reporting hasn't replaced shoe leather or the telephone, but it has helped news organizations to crunch large amounts of data and discern patterns that were previously invisible. In that sense, much about journalism's watchdog function has changed. If the adage of Watergate reporting was to "follow the money," we have many more ways to do so now. For all the talk television, tabloids and celebrity coverage, technology is a heavy counterweight for news organizations that know how to use it — and most do.

Stories about bank red-lining in San Francisco, police misconduct in New York City or health hazards of the hog industry in North Carolina have relied on computer analysis of public records.

In Raleigh, N.C., for example, *The News & Observer* won the 1996 Pulitzer Gold Medal for Public Service for its series, "Boss Hog," which traced the environmental risks posed by the state's growing hog-farming industry. Frank A. Daniels III, who was editor at the time, set up tools that allowed reporters to create their own searches and monitor public agencies, especially the legislature. Hurricane Floyd and the floods in its wake last September verified the newspaper's findings in horrific fashion. Practices brought to light in the newspaper's cautionary tale had indeed compromised the state water supply.

Effect No. 5: Digitization speeds up news coverage

The speed with which news travels from the street into the home is a function of digital technology. This is a bad thing when stories aren't properly verified. Usually, it's a good thing because consumers get more news, faster. To cite a few examples:

• An AP photographer's picture of 1996 presidential candidate Robert J. Dole falling from a stage reached headquarters 10 seconds later.

• World events, even wars, reach us live on television or the Internet as troops land or fight and as missiles explode.

• Print reporters write stories on laptops that can be transmitted from the scene, quickly edited and posted on the newspaper's Web site hours before the print edition rolls off the press.

In their book "Warp Speed," authors Bill Kovach and Tom Rosenstiel lament that this "all-news, all-the-time" environment has created a new "mixed-media culture" in which "the classic function of journalism to sort out a true and reliable account of the day's events is being undermined. It is being replaced by the continuous news cycle, the growing power of sources over reporters, varying standards of journalism, and a fascination with inexpensive, polarizing argument."

That's one take, and there are others. As this report shows, the changes in news technology and practice are coupled with parallel changes in public consumption of news. While the multimedia push to be first with the news exists — and it is dynamically different from the "Extra" newspaper edition of old — it remains only one element of news today, if a controversial one at that.

Mixed-media culture has been around for nearly a century, only now it challenges the practices and values of daily newspapers as never before. An all-day news cycle is as old as the AP, causing CEO Louis D. Boccardi to say with a chuckle, "Everyone today is discovering 24-hour news. Well, hello!"

> **Editors ... take pride in their ability to sort through the daily barrage of information to create an intelligent and entertaining news package, one with both spinach and dessert. The public has different ideas, though, needing fewer full-service products in a self-service world.**

Effect No. 6: Search agents and friends reduce the editor's role

Conventional wisdom says any publication or broadcast should combine what people want to know with what they need to know. Editors in all media live by this adage, taking pride in their ability to sort through the daily barrage of information to create an intelligent and entertaining news package, one with both spinach and dessert.

The public has different ideas, though, needing fewer full-service products in a self-service world. Sophisticated news consumers don't need a full meal; they know where to go and why. Those with Internet access differ from the unwired masses in the ways they get information. Their interest peaks for breaking news, but they rely on weeklies and specialty publications for background on the big stories. They still rely on journalistic editing, but more for Sunday dinner than for everyday fare.

Here's another analogy: On the information superhighway, people drive their own cars. Public transportation — i.e., traditional, full-service media — takes longer and may not take them where they want to go.

Digital searching through software agents is the key to the self-service world. Agents find what we want and bring it to us. Increasingly powerful agent software runs Internet search engines such as AltaVista, Yahoo! and Lycos, shifting information control from producers to consumers.

Almost every large Internet service lets people "personalize" a home page to deliver specific features such as stock prices, local news, sports scores and national political coverage — all with a few clicks of a mouse. In this world, the editor, once archbishop of information, recedes in importance.

Referrals by friends and family provide a different sorting function, a process described by economist Hal R. Varian, dean of the new School of Information and Management Systems at the University of California at Berkeley. By this evolving process, Internet users can rank stories they like and forward them to friends. The recipient can evaluate the offering based on how well the sender knows him, what this friend sent before, and how the sender's tastes compare with his own. A group of friends can form its own editorial brain trust.

This is a new, more personal information-sifting process — one tailored more closely to individuals. Its scope might not be as broadly civic as professional editors' "should-know" offerings. Yet again, it might be the same — just operating on a different time frame. We no longer have to debate these issues. We can just watch where the eyeballs go.

Effect No. 7: E-commerce brings on "collaborative filtering" and the "creepy factor"

The newest way to follow the eyeballs: clicking habits. Internet browsers record what we do online and make that data available to market researchers.

The great promise of online commercial markets lies in companies' ability to identify likely customers. Identifying the "right" users is a bit of a digital treasure hunt. Clustering software, often called "collaborative filtering," finds them.

When amazon.com e-mails you a notice that a particular author has a new book out, it has used collaborative filtering to analyze your book-buying habits and compare them with others of like habit. From all that information, the bookseller recommends a purchase with some confidence, even if you have never bought a book by that author online.

Collaborative filtering builds upon decades of marketing expertise about consumer behavior. Businesses have done this kind of thing for years in other arenas. For example, in the late 1980s, Volvo knew that its best potential buyer owned a 5-year-old Peugeot, so it relied on vehicle-registration records to identify new prospects.

Also, any entity interested in governance or civic issues has traditionally sought out members of public broadcasting stations. The interested solicitors included newspaper subscription departments and political parties.

This older targeting method was called affinity marketing because it could help sell a product based on related, yet independent, factors or interests. It was data-driven but less sophisticated than today's marketing, which analyzes millions of daily decisions with the new sorting and clustering software.

Yet, for all its promise, collaborative filtering has major limitations:

• Its reach exceeds its grasp. On a basic level, it often tells sellers what they already know about their customers.

• The ability to make direct solicitations has drawbacks. Customers who think a business "knows too much" about them might protest the invasion of privacy instead of buying a product. MSNBC.com uses collaborative filtering to identify groups, not individuals. "People assume anything you send them that they didn't ask for is creepy," said Steven J. White, Microsoft's director of product planning and research. "We strive for a low 'creepy factor.' ... With us, everything you get, you ask for. We ask, 'Would you like to see what other people who view news like you watch?' And we only send it if they say yes."

• For all the hype, collaborative filtering is not especially accurate. "Collaborative filtering is great in finding out things that are very obvious," said Edward K. Jung, former general manager of the Semantics Platform at Microsoft.

• The cost of improving this technology is huge, Jung said. Marketers must develop new software technologies and algorithms. Each incremental improvement often costs more than it brings in. "Collaborative filtering works in two cases: When it's very inexpensive to be wrong or when having a small improvement in sales is worth a lot," Jung said.

While many commercial opportunities exist online, they are tricky for advertising-based businesses, MSNBC's White said.

The robust marketplace of the Internet, then, offers a more textured opportunity for information providers with a few new tools. Some companies are reluctant to use them. Even those who do often find that Internet analysis is less effective than they had hoped, at least for now.

Effect No. 8: "Millennium bug" fixes have upgraded the digital infrastructure

In a world of unintended consequences, Y2K remediation brought some surprise benefits. Large media companies spent as much as 1% of revenues to make sure their computers know that this year is 2000, not 1900.

Despite a mostly uneventful transition, one benefit is clear: By investing in hardware and software to solve the Y2K problem, media companies also improved their digital news capabilities.

"About half of our properties got new front-end systems because of Year 2000" remediation, said Mindi Keirnan, senior vice president and general manager of the *San Jose Mercury News* and former vice president of Knight Ridder. The company had to "fast-forward several decisions we would have spread out if not for the millennium problem."

"The pressure came from having to decide whether to make a $500,000 patch or invest in a $2 million front-end system. From an efficiency point of view, it was sometimes cheaper to manage operations with people rather than machines," Keirnan said.

But the digital hardware gives Knight Ridder properties more design and new-product capabilities, she added. It also creates an infrastructure for database management that allows the company to use news again and again —

"repurposed," in the current lexicon.

Broadcast properties are experiencing a similar boon as they upgrade their signals for high-definition television (HDTV). And while the two terms are not necessarily synonymous, virtually all high-definition investments are in digital formats.

Effect No. 9: Digitization fuels e-commerce

As often happens with new inventions, digital information technology grew first in business applications and affected consumer activities later. Digital coding revolutionized the grocery business, for example, by changing inventory control and warehousing patterns to the advantage of large corporations and to the detriment of mom-and-pop stores. Likewise, the marriage of digitized information and Internet search capabilities has reshaped the news business.

Forrester Research and Jupiter Communications, which track Internet trends, show huge growth in the clicks-and-mortar world of e-commerce:

• Book and CD sales, travel bookings, grocery shopping and auctions are exploding on the Internet.

• U.S. retail sales are projected to increase from $18 billion in 1999 to $108 billion in 2003. (Even with that increase, online transactions would represent only 6% of retail sales.)

• Classified advertising is projected to grow from about $500 million in 1999 to $1.5 billion in 2002. While advertising doesn't count as retail commerce, many newspaper Web sites are extending their franchises to include real-estate brokerage services and financial services; job fairs and résumé screening; and financing and sales of cars and trucks.

• Transactions by businesses are projected to more than double, growing from $109 billion in 1999 to $251 billion in 2000. Computer upgrades comprise half of these sales, with automotive vehicles a distant second.

The Internet may drive sales but it appears to complement, not replace, those bricks-and-mortar businesses selling goods rather than information or services. Warehousing, delivering and exchanging items are some of the offline issues confronting online businesses. They're among the reasons amazon.com has yet to turn a profit while expanding its product lines to attract customers.

Effect No. 10: With signal compression comes HDTV, exponential choices

As with Y2K remediation, the FCC requirement that all TV stations transmit digital signals by 2006 has spurred major investments in digital equipment that will improve stations' flexibility. The top 10 markets had to convert by 1999.

High-definition television, in its most sophisticated formats, promises to provide the equivalent of 3-D movies for the small screen. But three standards are being adopted, and sets able to capture the enhanced signals are expensive.

The high-definition rollout puzzles consumers and companies alike. Why buy the sets if no transmissions exist? Why transmit when no one has the sets? Nevertheless, change is coming because high-definition capability enhances spectrum use. Stations can either broadcast multiple signals of programming or data at once — or one high-definition signal.

Federal policy clearly supports the improved visual experience of high-definition. But in the interim, and outside of prime time, the news could benefit from the change.

With a divisible signal, Mark Thalhimer of the Radio and Television News Directors Foundation said, "The potential exists for all local news stations to become providers of 24-hour local news."

The Internet

• All that traditional news organizations have to do to survive the digital era is to transfer their content to the Internet.

REALITY:
• America Online, the Internet's largest news provider, draws much of that news from traditional publishers or broadcasters, but customers' direct relationship is with AOL.

• While three of every four Internet users get news online, most seek information first from portal and search-engine sites rather than from established news brands. Traditional news-media companies are just developing their Web sites' capabilities as portals.

• The best commercial opportunities conflict with existing product strategies at traditional media companies.

ISSUES:
• For information providers the Internet battleground is not over content but conduit: Who controls customer access?

• Those who best aggregate information attract the audience and thus the commercial power. Information originators don't have the power, at least not now. AOL has no reporters and as many as 30 editors, depending on the news flow. *The Wall Street Journal* has 650 news professionals. AOL has 21 million paying subscribers; the *Journal* has about 1.8 million to its newspaper and 300,000 online.

• While the Internet provides a growing market for commercial transactions, its stand-alone business viability is unclear for information providers, with the exception of portals (such as AOL, Yahoo! or AltaVista), pornography peddlers and certain specialized information sites. Archive access might provide one revenue stream. The top 10 Web sites account for two-thirds of online advertising revenue.

TRENDS:
• Internet users have different news and media-consumption habits than the population as a whole:

• They watch more cable news, less network television.

• They read fewer daily newspapers but more weekly, business and science publications.

• Prime-time users of AOL would equal 6% of the adult TV audience — more than the UPN, WB and most cable networks draw.

• Ten percent of adults now go straight to the Internet for breaking news, compared with just under 40% each for broadcast and cable TV.

• More than half of all Internet users watch television while they are online.

• New devices and appliances enter the market regularly, increasing our connections to each other and to the Internet.

WATCH FOR THIS:
• The growth of broadband connections will determine how quickly media converge. By current estimates, 25% of homes will be wired by 2002.

• While cable leads the way in broadband development, start-up companies that lease and enhance phone lines are developing an alternative connection, called DSL for "digital subscriber lines."

• News producers will form more partnerships with portal sites.

• Web sites and other Internet-related

firms will spend billions of dollars to advertise in traditional, offline print and broadcast media.

• Programmers will develop new encoding languages to make searching for information or customers more precise. This development is expensive, though, while likely to yield only incremental gains.

• Internet services might gain rights to retransmit broadcast and cable programs, including news.

• The government and consumers will voice more privacy concerns, constraining the wired world.

• The Internet will become a bigger part of the bricks-and-mortar world as online transactions increase product demand, manufacture and delivery.

• Despite the Internet's promise of effectiveness and efficiency, e-commerce growth will be uneven. New technology diffusion is never perfect.

TOP NEWS / INFORMATION / ENTERTAINMENT WEB SITES
February 2000

Rank	Largest number of visitors	Unique visitors in a given month (000s)
1.	AOL News Channel	14,303
2.	AOL Entertainment Channel	11,385
3.	ZDNet	9,535
4.	About.com	9,339
5.	AOL Sports Channel	9,256
6.	AOL Computing Channel	8,874
7.	MSNBC.com	8,570
8.	CNET.com	8,280
9.	Weather.com	7,552
10.	Disney Online	6,016
11.	Go2Net.com	5,301
12.	FreeLotto.com	5,263
13.	Pathfinder.com	5,188
14.	iVillage Sites	5,002
15.	CNN.com	4,957

Source: Media Metrix

CHAPTER 2

Distribution: Give Us Your Eyeballs and Your Ears

I t's an age-old riddle: If a tree falls in a forest and no one hears it, does it make a sound?

Let's ask the question in media terms: If news happens, and no one distributes it, does it matter? What's more important: content or distribution?

The newsroom's answer is clear: "It's the content, stupid," declared pins on newspaper editors at industry meetings in the 1990s. But the marketplace's answer also resounds: Distribution rules.

Henry David Thoreau complained about this concerning the electronic telegraph connecting Maine to Texas more than a century ago. "What if Maine and Texas have nothing to say to each other?" he wondered.

As it turns out — through the telegraph, telephone, mass-market newspapers, magazines, radio, television and the Internet — Maine, Texas and the whole country have plenty to say to each other.

Content may come first, but it comes best with effective distribution. Humans want news. The business of news lies in the transaction, the distribution, of news.

Every business outside of manufacturing is working feverishly to keep the distribution horse before the content cart. Retailers, financial-service providers, telecommunications companies and media companies all define their businesses first by a customer base — the bigger and more diverse, the better. Grab their attention. Lock them in. Figure out what to sell them — what to put in the cart — later.

The idea of a "core" business has become quaint: "Bookseller" amazon.com is also the CD seller, videotape merchant, software dealer, home-improvement center, online auction house and specialty retailer — each line built on the size and strength of this channel to a huge pool of customers. Despite mounting losses from its expanding product lines, amazon.com plans to invest even more to attract customers.

These trends have pushed media companies into the fray:

• Media competition created limitless information and entertainment choices.

• Infinite new choices caused mass-media audiences to fracture.

• Federal deregulation of telecommunications and media ownership created efficiency and profit incentives.

• Media convergence means that electronic horsepower will pull the digitized information carts of the future. More and more information will flow through a screen — and not necessarily a TV screen.

How the news fits in remains unclear. But those who claim there is too much news have it backward. If anything, the explosion in distribution channels exceeds our capacity to flow content through the pipeline. We have so many horses sitting around that we hook them to the same cart. All-Monica television, the *Star's* Frank Gifford adultery scam, scaremongering network newsmagazines — they're all symptoms, but of what?

Media critics say sensational stories represent a decline from traditional standards. Historically, they do not. They're just modern manifestations of the age-old battle between news of importance and news of interest, flowing through an evolving system. We're still building the roads. We're still designing and making the new vehicles.

Those who fail to understand the dynamic pay dearly. Ask ABC or CBS News. Both passed on the opportunity to gain cable spectrum for expanded news operations. Now they compete with CNN, MSNBC and the Fox News Channel. It's too expensive to enter the cable-news game now as a stand-alone entity. Yet, the Internet or the next big thing might change the game again in a few years.

The Changing Audience: Classic Triangulation vs. the New Fragmentation

News is a derivative product. News is a trustworthy draw for a curious public, and for at least 100 years the press's business was its reading audience. Readers' subscriptions paid the cost of distribution. With the advent of advertising, the news became another kind of business.

Today, advertisers account for about 80% of newspaper revenues, with readers paying the balance through subscriptions and single-copy purchases. For broadcasters, advertisers pay it all, and viewers "pay" with their scarce time and attention. Cable's formula splits the cost differently because viewers pay for cable, but advertisers still do much of the heavy lifting.

Here's the classic model: News is distributed to grab the audience, which draws the advertising — that's triangulation. For most of the 20th century, this indirect business relationship with readers or viewers has not been a

> **Those who claim there is too much news have it backward. If anything, the explosion in distribution channels exceeds our capacity to flow content through the pipeline.**

problem for news organizations engaged in aggressive coverage of current events. The large capital investments necessary to own a media franchise — a printing press, a broadcast transmitter, a wired community — kept competition scarce and audiences robust. Limited choice kept audiences and advertising dollars channeled toward a few places.

Media dynamics changed as technologies emerged. The total market grew, but each new medium altered audience behavior and changed the distribution mix. In the United States:

- Two-thirds of homes subscribe to cable TV, projected to reach 70% by 2002.
- Daily newspapers penetrate just over half of U.S. households, compared with nearly all in the 1960s.
- All homes have televisions, but only one-third tune into the prime-time "Big Three" network programming that a generation ago captured nine out of 10 viewers.
- Viewers spend about as much time watching cable TV as they do broadcast programs.
- More than half of U.S. homes have computers. One-third also have Internet access.
- Internet users read more newsweeklies and business publications but fewer newspapers on weekdays, according to Forrester Research.
- Almost half of online users simultaneously watch television at home, and about 6% of households are online during prime time.

The good news for media companies is that despite a fractured audience, ad expenditures remain robust in these booming times. With so much competition, even a smaller "mass" audience still has value. This could change because:

- Daily newspaper ad revenue continues to grow, but the medium's share of the whole advertising pie continues to decline.
- Dailies also see a softness in linage for help-wanted classified advertising,

their most profitable ad segment.

• A growing amount of traditional classified advertising is moving to the Internet, where search capabilities and other services provide a new marketplace for those seeking a job or buying a house or car.

• Network broadcasters have continued to enjoy robust revenue despite shrinking audiences, although rates have declined.

• TV audiences are tiring of the increased program time devoted to advertising. What does this mean for distribution?

NBC was among the first to understand this last point and use it to audience advantage, most notably on its "Today" show, said Andrew R. Lack, president of NBC News. "Today," No. 1 in the morning-news contest, starts right after the local news signs off and contains no commercials for the first 22 minutes. It makes up commercial time later in the program, when the audience shifts away from those running out the door to work. "NBC Nightly News" follows a similar formula.

"We want to give the viewer as few choices as possible to change the channel," Lack said of the practice, now copied by other morning news shows.

In the fall 1999 prime-time season, CBS and ABC increased commercial time per program. NBC and the WB network did not; instead, they commanded premium rates — in NBC's case, for more desirable demographics and, for the WB, a growing audience.

Capturing and keeping audience attention is a requirement in media distribution. Doing so successfully is the currency of commerce, no matter what the business. For media businesses, especially the news business, it is crucial.

How Market Changes Affect News Distribution

The fracturing audience flies squarely in the face of 20th-century media economics, where size matters.

Economists note that news and information are unlike other products because they are expensive to produce but relatively inexpensive to reproduce. That, more than anything, determines how they are sold.

As Professor Hal Varian of the University of California-Berkeley, an adviser to this project, noted in his new book, "Information Rules":

"The cost of producing the first copy of an information good may be substantial, but the cost of producing (or reproducing) additional copies is negligible. This sort of cost structure has many important implications. For example, cost-based pricing just doesn't work: A 10-20% markup on unit cost makes no sense when unit cost is zero. You must price your information goods according to consumer value, not according to your production costs."

For the news-media business, that means selling (or giving) news to audiences for whatever they will pay, then leveraging the quality and size of that audience to make the real money from advertisers. In this world, for example, young women attract more ad dollars than middle-age or older women because they spend more on the items most mass-market advertisers sell.

For TV stations, ratings are the audience measure. For newspapers and other publications, it is circulation. For the Internet, it is "unique viewers" and "page views," which measure how long a visitor looks at a Web site.

Let's look at the concept of scale and how it can change the way new information media develop over time. One example, from television:

In the early days of television, the FCC awarded many TV licenses to newspaper publishers. The government assumed that newspapers, as trustworthy institutions in their communities, would fill the airwaves with "public-interest," local, civic-based news of the type they published in their newspapers.

It was a good idea, just not economically sound. TV production costs were so great that a local market was too small to be profitable at the time. Advertisers would not pay enough for the small numbers of local households to cover local news-production costs.

When that became clear, in the 1950s, the FCC reversed the policy. Later, in the 1970s, it banned publishers from owning TV stations in their own markets. A network-centered news system developed — dominated by ABC, CBS and NBC — that held firm for more than a quarter of the century.

But with population growth, markets and costs changed again. Now cheaper, easier, local TV news is the rule. Today, profitability doesn't depend on a national scale. Local TV news now drives station profits. "The local station with the best news program has the best overall ratings," said Edward L. Scanlon, executive vice president of NBC.

Realizing that market forces are shifting yet again, the FCC is looking at lifting its ban on local newspaper-television cross-ownership. The change would support robust local reporting by spreading its cost and audience over more than one medium to compete in the new wired world.

The scale sequence — local experiments, going national, then local again — is playing out anew in the Internet era. Search-engine and content providers like Yahoo! have worked first to build a national audience whose attention will support news, information and entertainment of any kind and, second, to improve quality by adding local partners. Should it play out as in the past, this process could help news organizations from old media, if they can remain robust through the transition.

Print Media Face the Biggest Distribution Problem

As important as content quality, sometimes more so, is the quality of the distribution system that sells and delivers the information. Benjamin Franklin knew this when, as the nation's first postmaster, he established low-cost mail

> **As important as content quality, sometimes more so, is the quality of the distribution system that sells and delivers the information. ... The problems are most acute for U.S. daily newspapers, with their time-pressed delivery and somewhat archaic sales practices.**

delivery of colonial newspapers, several of which he owned himself!

Franklin, of course, was ahead of his time. Nowhere has distribution proved more important than for newspapers and magazines. The problems are most acute for U.S. daily newspapers, with their time-pressed delivery and somewhat archaic sales practices.

Still, many journalists believe that the public rushes to scoop up newspapers only if they are great. They used to be great in great numbers, the myth goes, and that's why they dominated the scene. It is a romantic notion. Many successful newspapers of yesteryear were awful.

Today, slightly more than half the nation's households buy newspapers, fewer than those paying for cable TV. If news quality alone determines audience, how does one explain wrestling as the most popular on-cable programming?

Like it or not, the way people get news and information — the ease and efficiency of delivery — can make or break a news enterprise.

It is worthwhile to look at how U.S. newspapers manage circulation. For most of the 20th century, trucks shipped copies to children, who sold them on corners or delivered them on bicycles. But as dailies shifted from afternoon to morning editions, delivered before dawn, adults in cars replaced the kids.

When the kids disappeared, the customer relationship became less personal. Service levels often declined. No neighborhood waifs at the door selling subscriptions or collecting. No parents to call if a kid missed a delivery. Cancellations grew. Newspapers created impersonal phone banks to sell new, mostly discounted subscriptions. Nonpayments grew. More subscriptions were sold, more discounts given.

The problem is called "churn." Magazines experience similar subscription turnover, but the task of managing sales for dailies dwarfs that of weekly and monthly publications, even when content is good.

Most publications have two classes of readers: a cadre of loyal, longtime subscribers who depend on the paper or magazine; and the churn, those attracted with discounts and other incentives who cancel when the premiums end.

With few exceptions today, most publishers aim each year to sign up as many new subscribers as total circulation, reported by the Audit Bureau of Circulations. For example, a 100,000-circulation newspaper might have 50,000 loyal subscribers but would have to sign up 100,000 more each year to keep the "churning" 50,000 replenished.

In short, newspaper readership is akin to filling a bathtub with no plug. The volume flowing in must at least match that flowing out or the level recedes. The cost of this practice is enormous.

Equally important in the circulation equation are managing customer lists, keeping up with mobility in the market and collecting subscription fees. Youth carriers did it all. Not all newspapers do it so diligently today.

While database marketing is evolving, most large-newspaper publishers complain that no off-the-shelf system right now ties good subscriber information to delivery systems.

Gannett Co., the nation's largest newspaper owner with 74 dailies, created its own proprietary market database system. The program helps manage both circulation and advertising sales while measuring the growth opportunity of potential acquisitions.

The Dallas Morning News, The Arizona Republic in Phoenix and *The Orange County* (Calif.) *Register* also use sophisticated systems to target residents for subscriptions as well as delivery of other publications and advertising circulars, giving advertisers one-stop distribution service in those markets.

Through 1999, such programs had mixed results. Daily circulation increased at newspapers with circulations over 500,000 but decreased, by 0.5% to 1.5%, in every other category, according to a Newspaper Association of America analysis of September 1999 publishers' statements. Sunday circulation declined in all circulation categories.

As for the Gannett dailies, at least one-third gained circulation. In 1999 the *Republic* grew Sunday but declined weekdays. The *Register* gained on weekdays but not Sunday. The *Morning News,* allowing no circulation discounts, declined in all categories.

Collecting subscription payments is increasingly difficult. More newspapers bill by mail — sometimes quarterly, sometimes every four weeks to eke out a "13th month" of payment. Few discount long-term advance payments, a practice that arguably could reduce collection overhead and churn. The conventional wisdom: Why give discounts to readers willing to pay full price?

Compare those practices with some online companies that give a free computer to customers who sign up for a three-year connection subscription. The profit comes from lower marketing costs to get new subscribers plus higher advertising rates for a guaranteed audience base.

In contrast, newspaper publishers give subscribers many more monthly or quarterly opportunities than other media to end the business relationship through nonpayment. Customers pay annually for magazine subscriptions and in advance for books.

The Washington Post maintains its large, paid D.C.-area penetration (48% daily and 56% Sunday) through a massive effort using both new and old systems, Publisher Donald E. Graham said. Subscribers can pay in advance by mail.

Just in case they don't, the *Post's* field force goes door-to-door to collect, just as youth carriers once did. This system is key to the *Post's* penetration success, but few major dailies have adopted it. Boisfeuillet Jones Jr., the *Post's* president, general manager and associate publisher, explained it this way: "Our biggest concern is readership. It permeates everything else we do."

The *Post* also understands how price-sensitive newspaper buyers can be. So its Monday-through-Saturday newsstand price is still 25 cents — virtually free, given what a quarter buys these days.

Managing a paid circulation base can be more trouble than it's worth, especially for weeklies. *The Village Voice,* for example, shifted from mostly paid to free circulation in 1996. In the process, the recently sold New York weekly more than doubled its circulation base — from 112,000 to nearly 250,000 — with enough of an ad-revenue boon to profitably forego some $3 million in circulation revenue.

The New York Times created a customer "membership": a credit card for subscriptions, discounted meals and services, and special members-only events such as authors' luncheons. This aims to strengthen the customer relationship so subscribers will go to the *Times* first for news and other information needs.

Various media programs around the country have the same goal — holding onto the customer relationship, measured in newspapers by circulation, in broadcast by viewership, and on Web sites by visits and page views.

It is that customer relationship that has greatest value. When my family sold *The Oakland Tribune* in 1992 to the Alameda Newspaper Group, that's what we sold: our relationships. Advertising contracts, subscriptions and delivery infrastructure — not presses or buildings — were all that passed to a competing publisher of four other dailies. Although the *Tribune's* audited circulation exceeded that of the four others combined, the buyer measured its market value only by its customer relationships and distribution system. Never was that formulation more of a driving force than it is today.

Don't Have Distribution? Buy It!

No scorecard could keep up with the frantic pace of mergers and acquisitions among telecom and media companies following the 1996 Telecommunications Act. This law sought to promote local-service competition. Other media consolidated outside the law's reach. In the last year alone:

• Long-distance carrier AT&T Corp. acquired giant cable operator Tele-Communications Inc., and together they moved to buy MediaOne, another cable behemoth. AT&T Corp. also inked deals with Time Warner Inc. and Microsoft Corp. to provide phone or interactive services via cable modem and television. It also signed an exclusive contract with Internet-service and broadband provider Excite@Home to offer high-speed cable access to the Internet.

• MCI WorldCom Inc. acquired long-distance carrier Sprint Corp. for $115 billion, which with the requisite approvals would become the biggest deal ever made.

• CBS agreed to merge with media conglomerate Viacom.

• America Online announced its intention to merge with Time Warner Inc. It also acquired CompuServe, a weak competitor; Netscape, the Web browser concern; and MovieFone, the information and theater-ticket company. It continues to deal with long-distance and local phone-service providers for high-speed Internet connections.

• Disney/ABC invested in Go Network, which includes the Infoseek browser.

• Amazon.com continued to expand its retail-product base by acquiring drugstore.com and pets.com. In November, it announced it would add toys, software and home-improvement merchandise to its offerings.

• The Hearst Corp., publisher of the *San Francisco Examiner*, bought out its competitor under a joint-operating arrangement, the *San Francisco Chronicle* — consolidating newspaper ownership in the nation's fourth largest media market. The transaction is under legal challenge, however.

• A.H. Belo Corp., parent of *The Dallas Morning News,* merged its Internet and broadcast operations in Dallas, Houston and San Antonio to create the Texas Cable Network, patterned after a less ambitious regional network in the Pacific Northwest.

• Tribune Co. agreed to acquire Times Mirror, making it the second largest broadcast and third largest newspaper company in the United States.

The list could go on. It excludes any number of newspaper mergers and swaps, meant to bulk up distribution in defined geographic areas, as Gannett has done in New Jersey and MediaNews Group did in California. The deals all try to achieve economies of scale and to increase revenue from advertising and other services.

Conduit Providers vs. Content Providers
The flip side of these gigantic telecom customer bases is the enormous investment to upgrade systems for high-speed information delivery. It's called

broadband: permanent, online connections at speeds between 256k and 1.5 million bits per second. Conventional phone connections reach a maximum speed of 56k bps. Higher-speed lines have not been readily available to homes, and they are more expensive than most cable-TV or telecommunications service — from $60 to $110 per month. Yet they provide instant Internet access and pull in software, sound and video in a flash. If connected by cable, broadband eliminates the need for multiple phone lines.

In the end, the speed and size of the wire (or its wireless equivalent) will expand the distribution system exponentially. Broadband delivery will finally bring home the promised media convergence.

What has held up the digital renaissance has been the expense of building home connections to the telecommunications network of wires and wireless relays. That gap in service is called "the last mile."

Traditionally, cable companies' fat wires had great capacity but lacked switching for interactive, two-way communication. Phone companies had the switches but limited wiring capacity. Now, phone and cable mergers allow for major investments to build out an interactive system.

Cable companies have moved more aggressively to position themselves as the broadband leaders. They still have the advantage, although upstart entrepreneurs are creating local digital subscriber line (DSL) Internet access through leased telephone lines.

An important new wrinkle in the broadband expansion concerns what regulators call "common carriage." Which entities must make their home lines broadly available to content and service providers?

Traditionally, the government regulated telephone and cable companies as common carriers: classified as natural monopolies because their capital costs made competition prohibitively expensive. To ensure the building of these systems, the FCC and local regulators granted exclusive licenses in specific markets. In return, the telecom companies had to make their wires available to anyone at an affordable price.

The wrinkle came in 1985, when federal courts ruled that cable companies are not simple common carriers. As TV-program providers, cable operators had the same First Amendment rights as publishers, the court ruled. With sole control over their program lineups, cable operators could include or exclude anything — even network programming.

Years of legal wrangling ensued, and a new regulatory framework grew to ensure that broadcast programming remained available to the two-thirds of U.S. homes with cable service — and later, to homes with satellite TV connections.

More recently, limited access to cable carriage has thwarted the plans of more than one TV programmer or news provider. ABC, for example, dropped plans for a 24-hour cable news network because it could not sign up enough

> **The short-term trends create audience access issues for old-line information gatekeepers, especially news companies, as electronic delivery threatens to subsume and overwhelm their traditional, though powerful, distribution systems.**

local cable operators to make it financially viable. Barry Diller, CEO of USA Network, failed to convert shopping channels to news channels.

The tightening competition for cable "shelf space" has shifted the balance of power between cable operators and TV programmers. More often than not, new cable channels either are paying cable operators for carriage or making them equity partners in the channel.

In the mythical 500-channel world, such scarcity would not be a problem. But such a world, if it develops at all, can only bring more headaches for programmers. The biggest issue, of course, would be how to draw viewers to a channel. Web-site operators already face this problem as they scramble to establish potent brand identities.

In the meantime, access to cable spectrum will only tighten further with the addition of high-definition signals.

The Real Media Superpowers

If the FCC approved all the pending convergence deals, three cable companies and two telephone operators could wire the entire nation. Current law requires only phone companies to make their wires available to all. Cable companies have choices.

Among the looming policy questions:

• Does signing up for a phone or cable service lock you into a specific Internet provider?

• Can a few companies limit Internet access as Microsoft tried to do by bundling its Explorer browser with its computer operating systems?

Already, AT&T, a cable and long-distance provider, is under pressure to offer its broadband network to the full range of Internet-service providers — despite its recent agreement to give exclusive cable broadband access to Excite@Home, which provides Internet networking services and a portal with

16 million home subscribers.

In contrast, the upstart DSL broadband providers serve customers through regulated telephone wires.

Until the resolution, AT&T Chairman Michael Armstrong advocates more separation between Internet content and transmission services to lessen regulatory problems. Armstrong would rather grow household share than fight a political war over AT&T's role as an information gatekeeper. No one knows whether the other emerging telecom behemoths would give up vertical integration of content and distribution. This movement remains in vogue because it assures big markets for content providers, from news organizations to filmmakers.

No matter the outcome, the short-term trends create audience access issues for old-line information gatekeepers, especially news companies, as electronic delivery threatens to subsume and overwhelm their traditional, though powerful, distribution systems.

The New Gatekeeper: The First Screen

Here's how fragmented media converge: You sign up for broadband access to infinite variety on the Internet. Simply by turning on your preferred device — be it telephone, computer, television or some hybrid — the first screen pops up. Everyone sees it, and everyone wants to be on it.

The first screen is not the traditional front page. In fact, no list of the most popular Web sites includes any traditional news provider, even though 73% of Web visitors surveyed said they call up news online. News ranks third in online use, following research and e-mail to family and friends, an AOL survey found.

A Media Metrix survey in August 1999 ranked AOL news, sports and other services as four of the top five entertainment and news sites. Coming in seventh, MSNBC was the first recognizable news brand in unique visitors. CNN came in second among news sites, 14th overall.

Online users usually visit the top online brands the most. Leading this list are the "portals" or "aggregators" — the big sites with powerful search engines, great marketing and huge capitalization: AOL, Yahoo!, MSN (Microsoft Network), Lycos, amazon.com, Weather.com, Disney. All of them garner millions of visitors monthly. The AOL News Channel claims to attract almost 14 million individuals each month. Its strong brand name aces out mostly local U.S. news organizations. *The New York Times* took a century to build a brand name in news. AOL took a decade, not hiring a single reporter but distributing the *Times* and dozens of other news providers.

For publishers and traditional broadcasters, the media-gatekeeper concept is changing radically. Information providers must navigate an increasingly mediated system that includes:

- Telecommunications connections.
- Internet service providers.
- The first screen: a browser or portal site that appears instantly when connections are complete.
- Finally, one or more links to the news provider's own Web site.

Broadband services will collapse this hierarchy, merging the wiring, service provider and portal into a seamless connection that is always on and ready to go. But who will control that first screen? And what will be on it?

The first screen is nothing less than the consumer's gateway to the information universe. Excite@Home, the cable broadband service, co-brands with other companies, creating sites such as Work.com with Dow Jones (a business user portal) and MySchwab (a personalized portal for investors). Real Cities, a Knight Ridder venture, co-brands with newspaper partners on local Web sites. So far, few others do. The balance could change, depending on mergers, partnerships, regulation or a host of other variables.

The new pathways to the former reader or viewer (or to their children) are an obstacle course for news-media companies, who can no longer control distribution of their own products.

Repackaging Network News:
The "Big Three," Fox and CNN

If any doubt remains over the importance of distribution, consider how the fortunes of broadcast network news today hinge on strategic decisions made years ago. Since the 1960s, television has been the nation's most heavily relied upon news source. Today, the largest and most profitable network news operation belongs to NBC, which picks up viewers:

• On its broadcast news programs: "Today," "NBC Nightly News" with Tom Brokaw and its prime-time magazine, "Dateline," which airs five nights a week.

• On CNBC, a mostly financial cable channel.

• On MSNBC, an all-news service, part of a cable and Internet joint venture with Microsoft.

• On its popular MSNBC Web site.

In addition, local NBC affiliates can order national or international stories packaged by a network-operated center in Charlotte, N.C., which gets news feeds from around the world and edits them on demand.

"We set up a system to look like a place where anyone can pop up anytime," explained anchor Tom Brokaw, who helped broker the NBC-Microsoft partnership. The system reinforces the NBC brand and "sells" the same news package to different advertisers and audiences, offsetting programming costs.

MSNBC rebroadcasts "Today." The "News with Brian Williams" airs at 9 p.m. on MSNBC and at 10 p.m. on CNBC. NBC repackages its archive via a growing list of cable magazines, the longest running of which is the news retrospective show, "Time and Again" with Jane Pauley.

How NBC built this system and why CBS and ABC chose not to do likewise highlights strategic and business priorities. The answers are key indicators of the future of news, as journalistic operations become "departments" of ever-larger corporate entities.

These networks with news operations consider them prestigious business assets. Over the years, the fortunes of the traditional "Big Three" have risen and fallen with ownership changes and other factors.

CBS, the "Tiffany network" that for decades set standards for network news, shrank in vision and size under Laurence Tisch's ownership from 1985 to 1995.

ABC, acquired by Disney in 1995, saw itself mostly as an entertainment entity. After Disney bought Capital Cities/ABC, it sold off its newspapers and magazines to concentrate on theme parks, movies, TV production, its ESPN cable sports channels and, more recently, Internet portals. ESPN is the most profitable cable channel. Disney Online ranks ninth in Media Metrix's list of top information and entertainment Web sites. Two other Disney Web ventures also rank in the worldwide top 10.

After the dust settled, neither ABC nor CBS had its own cable news channel.

The landscape was set in the early 1990s, following years of negotiations between broadcast networks and cable operators over the rights to, and value of, broadcast signals. The broadcasters successfully established the value of their programs to cable subscribers and operators. How much should the cable industry pay for the years of financial inequity?

CBS took cash, selling its cable holdings. ABC and NBC opted for new cable channels. ABC launched ESPN2 on its channel, reinforcing its dominance and financial prowess in sports. NBC had a different strategy, unclear at first.

The head of NBC's cable operations at the time was Thomas S. Rogers, who has since left NBC to run Primedia, mostly a publisher of consumer and business magazines. Rogers had been a staff lawyer for the congressional committee that wrote the 1986 cable deregulation act.

Under the First Amendment, cable operators had the right to determine how many news, sports, movie and other channels went into their lineups. Cable network programmers signed contracts specifying the nature of their programs and could change their offerings only with the cable operator's consent.

NBC decided that its strength was in news, relative to broadcast rivals who focused more on entertainment, Rogers said. The network was exploring an all-news channel to rival CNN but had not figured out how to develop or pay for it. At the time, Microsoft was in negotiations for a partnership with CNN, not NBC. So NBC created a soft-news channel called America's Talking, mostly featuring interviews and talking heads, Rogers said. He defined America's Talking in contracts with cable operators in a way that allowed NBC News to substitute an all-news MSNBC without having to renegotiate existing contracts for carriage.

As for ABC, it planned to offer an all-news cable channel, but by early 1998, with no partner and no clear chance of signing up enough cable systems — plus the advent of Disney ownership — the network dropped its plan. It has since reduced its news staff of correspondents and its overseas bureau operations.

Media czar Rupert Murdoch's News Corp. spent the 1990s investing heavily in a U.S. local and national news-distribution system. Commentators have called its 24-hour cable-news channel a politically conservative alternative for news, but Fox News Channel President Roger Ailes disagrees. "We said we were going to do fair and balanced news, and that scared them," he said. "We were adding points of view. That's the reason we got into this business. The issue is not bias. It's arrogance. Many believe that God created them to shove their points of view down the public's throat. There's no tolerance for other points of view."

In addition, Fox requires each local affiliate to develop a local newscast if they don't have one already. Fox is subsidizing the system's growth.

If fully developed, Fox will combine 24-hour cable news with a network affiliate system like NBC has. It has a Fox sports network, like ABC's ESPN, and is developing regional sports networks in major cable markets. While Fox has yet to mount a broadcast-network newscast, it is developing a system that would support such a program, one with enough distribution support to spread costs over Fox's national and international network.

For CNN's part, the cable-news pioneer has news-sharing relationships with local broadcast stations, but it lacks the formal affiliate relationships that would reinforce brand identity, reliably spread its costs or grow its revenue across cable and broadcast television platforms. It does have a strong world-wide general news channel and its Headline News channel in addition to sports and business networks.

Earlier in 1999, rumors flew that CNN would merge with CBS, creating the same kind of cable-network/local-affiliate distribution system that NBC has grown and Fox is building. CBS later agreed to merge with Viacom, and CNN — as part of Time Warner — became a jewel destined for the AOL crown. But a broadcast-cable network is not CNN's plan.

CNN is building an international and interactive news service instead. "We have no plans to compete with local broadcasters," said Eason Jordan, CNN's president of Newsgathering and International Networks. "We are a global news company. We compete globally. We have an unrivaled group of affiliates at the local (U.S.) level — three times greater than any network. We have contracts for "first pictures" with 630 broadcast stations. In some cases, we have contracts with every local station in a market that does news. We may get beaten on any given story, but in many cases we have a more compelling use of footage than the station does. The consortium of local television affiliates (set up by ABC, CBS and Fox) is meant to combat the CNN factor. We have two decades of advantage of having more than one feed.

"We added 400 people to our interactive unit. It's now the fastest growing part of our company. The AOL merger forces us to take another look at our strategy. There will be a convergence of broadcasting and interactive in the end. Those with the best programming and software will win. We have the best distribution in cable and are doing very well in interactive."

Daily Distribution:
Top Three Markets Plus the AP

Two national newspapers, *USA TODAY* and *The Wall Street Journal,* have the largest circulations among U.S. dailies. But both publish only on weekdays, and neither is anchored in a local community.

Dailies in the top three urban markets illustrate more clearly the intricate distribution strategies of this mostly local medium. Each faces local competition but leads its market in revenue and influence.

To end this series of distribution profiles, Associated Press CEO Louis D. Boccardi offers his perspective on distributing the news in a high-tech environment.

The New York Times model: a national-local hybrid
After unsuccessful efforts for decades, *The New York Times* has intensified its national distribution strategy. It publishes national and international reports, anchored by coverage of its home market. A strong brand identity adds to these other advantages:

• Of 1.1 million sales daily and 1.7 million Sunday, about 40% is sold outside the New York tri-state area.

• Choosing growth opportunities nationwide, rather than within a single geographic market, gives the *Times* financial flexibility that local and regional papers lack.

• As a leading national publication, the *Times* receives a larger share of its ad linage from national advertisers and a smaller share from classifieds, the category thought to be most vulnerable to Internet growth.

The Los Angeles Times model: growing at home
Executives at the nation's largest locally circulated newspaper, with 1.1 million readers, have been striving to deepen readership within its huge geographic and multiethnic market.

Two years ago, Mark H. Willes, then CEO of the parent Times Mirror Co., announced plans to increase circulation by 50% within three years. Few in the industry believed it possible, and the *Times* has not gotten near its goal. It reorganized coverage in some cases and invested in business news. Some circulation programs do show signs of adding circulation within the paper's defined market:

• To build readership through content, the *Times* launched local *Our Times* sections — 28 in all, some weekly, some daily — for areas no bigger than 10,000 subscribers each.

• Officials claim more than 100,000 in new sales through joint distribution arrangements with the Spanish-language daily *La Opinión* (of which the *Times* is part owner) and Sunday home delivery of the locally published *Korean Times*. Both ethnic publications carry the *Times* as an insert.

• The *Times* teamed up with rival daily publisher MediaNews Group to distribute advertising fliers to subscribers and nonsubscribers throughout the greater Los Angeles area.

• The strategies will be under review, as a result of the announced takeover of Times Mirror by Tribune Co.

The *Chicago Tribune* model: covering the multimedia bases

The *Tribune's* daily circulation of about 650,000, and more than 1 million on Sunday, is just one part of a local Tribune Co. empire that reaches its audience through several venues:

• Its broadcast station WGN, a WB network affiliate, ranks fourth in the greater Chicago market and has national reach through wide cable distribution.

• WGN radio and CLTV (ChicagoLand Television), its local all-news cable channel, add coverage and marketing synergies.

• The *Chicago Tribune* Web site is a regional portal to numerous services and information sources.

• Tribune Co. increases its sports presence with ownership of the Chicago Cubs and partnership in Fox's regional sports network.

Reporters from the newspaper regularly appear on the local TV, radio and cable programs. In fact, the *Tribune* installed a broadcast set, complete with lights and robotic cameras, in the middle of the newsroom.

Contracts to carry Chicago sporting events, including the Tribune Co.-owned Cubs, on television, radio and cable reinforce the *Tribune* brand and distribution with nonsubscribers. And the company's multiple media outlets create synergy and efficiency for the ad-sales staff, which can offer space throughout the local system.

Tribune Co.'s cross-ownership of newspaper and broadcast properties was grandfathered in before the federal ban. Newspapers in only a few markets, including San Francisco, Dallas and New York City, share this advantage. Tribune Co. is challenging the ban with its acquisition of Times Mirror, which would create cross-ownership in New York, Los Angeles and Hartford, as well as in Florida, where under a temporary FCC waiver it owns both the *Sun-Sentinel* in Fort Lauderdale and recently acquired WBZL, the Miami WB affiliate.

The Associated Press model: leveraging distribution

The AP, a nonprofit cooperative for its publishing and broadcasting members, built a news distribution system that could be a textbook success story.

Even as its chief competitor, United Press International, was collapsing years ago, the AP concluded that it had to step up to some challenges and that its biggest problem was its own success.

"All but six newspapers in the country were members," according to CEO Louis D. Boccardi.

With no natural place to grow, the news service knew it couldn't increase revenue by simply raising rates. Equally important, as it entered new business lines, it had to be careful not to undertake ventures in direct competition with its members. The AP's unique asset was a distribution system linking every news organization. The key was in adding value to that distribution system, as Boccardi explained:

• First, the AP boosted its members' technological capability with satellite dishes, electronic darkrooms and more recently an infrastructure allowing global transmission of digital photos within seconds after they are shot.

• It also turned its universal connection into a business distributing other wire services, syndicated wire material and advertising pages directly into newspaper production systems.

• With its knowledge of worldwide coverage, mostly in print but also in broadcast, it launched a television "wire" service for international clients.

• Its experience in developing news-industry technology earned the AP a $150 million contract to build editing and transmission systems for the BBC. Since then, others have purchased it as well, including ABC News.

• The AP's Web site provides more than 500 newspapers with some electronic services, including Web-site design.

As a result of these changes, about one-third of AP's $550 million in 1999 revenue came from new, for-profit ventures. Prices for basic services have stayed mostly flat, but additional services are available for those who want to buy them. One example: video packages for local Web sites.

Through it all, the AP's basic mission has remained intact. It still covers every state capital in the land, but its scale also allowed it to move from time-honored service to digital-news pioneer.

"The steps we're taking are to strengthen the cooperative, but we're also finding new revenue to strengthen AP's core mission," Boccardi said. "If we had stayed in the 'box' of cooperative, at some point we'd have to ask, 'Does this work anymore?'"

Newspapers

MYTHS:

• Newspapers will be potentially extinct because the American public doesn't read anymore.

• The Internet will put newspapers out of business.

REALITY:

• U.S. adults spend less time reading daily newspapers, but they read as much or more than ever — weekly newspapers and newsmagazines, Sunday newspapers, books and online information.

• The habit of reading weekly news publications is more prevalent among Internet users than nonusers and strengthens with online use.

• Internet development is brisk but uneven, pulling business from newspapers but creating opportunities as well. Historically, new media do not drive out the old. They add to the mix, sometimes pushing the weakest franchises out of business.

ISSUES:

• Can newspapers realign operations with the changing rhythms of news consumption and commerce?

• Can they make money meeting those new demands?

• Will new commercial arrangements compromise newspapers' integrity or public-service value?

• Can newspapers, with their low pay scales, attract and maintain talented staff during the dot-com stock market frenzy?

• Can newspapers re-establish a direct relationship with their customers in the digital world — a connection now mediated by an Internet world of service providers, browsers and portals?

TRENDS:

• Consumers' slow but steady shift to weekly newspaper readership is real, as these measurements show:

• Sunday readership is more prevalent among all readers, and more pronounced among Internet users, the

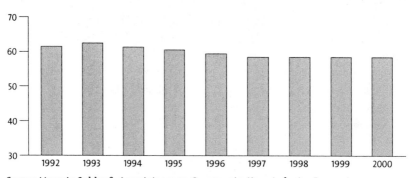

AGGREGATE CIRCULATION OF U.S. DAILY NEWSPAPERS (in millions)

Source: Veronis, Suhler & Associates 1999 Communications Industry Forecast

Newspaper Association of America found in its Fall 1999 Competitive Media Index analysis.

• *USA TODAY* now separates its Friday weekend-edition circulation reports from its Monday-Thursday figures to capitalize on the larger readership with higher advertising rates. Many daily newspapers report Sunday circulation separately for the same reason.

• The National Newspaper Association, which primarily represents weekly newspapers, shows weekly circulation growing by 3.3% a year — with free papers leading the pack.

• Despite newspapers' dominant role in reporting, even national papers do not drive Web traffic the way TV Web sites do.

• Newspapers are the major source of "new news," defined here as fresh information entering the global news stream. So any diminution of newspaper reporting threatens the amount of "new news" available to broadcast outlets as well, as these findings indicate in an NAA survey of television news professionals:

• Half of all TV journalists read at least three newspapers a day.

• Seventy percent of assignment editors read at least that many dailies, and nearly half read four or more per day.

• While broadcast journalists say they do not take news verbatim from newspapers, at least one-third of TV reporters and assignment editors used newspapers "often" or more frequently to decide what to cover.

• Broadcasts routinely lead with local and national enterprise reporting from newspapers.

• With a few notable exceptions, the newspaper franchise remains local, but most papers have yet to fully use this advantage to integrate information and advertising operations with digital information services.

• The ethnic and foreign-language press is vigorous, growing and forming partnerships with metropolitan dailies.

• The largest new source of newspaper revenue comes from Internet-company advertising. Online businesses, vying for top-of-mind name recognition in the fragmented Internet market, spent $2 billion in 1999 on newspaper ads, $1 billion in the fourth quarter alone. That spending is projected to reach $3 billion in 2000. (Spending accelerated markedly since the first half of 1999, during which online advertisers spent only $108 million on newspaper ads, about twice that on network television advertising, and $755 million on a combination of "radio, other television, print and outdoor ads.")

• Classified advertising is shifting to the Internet, largely at the expense of newspapers, as these trends show:

• By 2003, an estimated $2.8 billion — 27% of all Internet ad expenditures — will be for classifieds.

• Newspapers' most profitable segment — recruitment, or help-wanted, ad revenue — is moving most quickly to the Internet, but automotive and real estate sales find key efficiencies there as well.

• This online advertising includes selling additional products and services such as financing and brokerage services.

• These new online advertising activities sometimes cause newspapers and their Web sites to compete against themselves or their advertisers and their Web sites.

• But some pioneering Internet classified advertisers find they still need newspapers to augment Web traffic.

WATCH FOR THIS:

• The FCC, Congress or the courts could relax cross-ownership rules governing newspapers and local TV stations. Newspapers might benefit greatly from a change like one the commission approved last fall, which allowed broadcast companies to buy other TV and radio stations in the same market. Repealing the newspaper-broadcast ownership rules would increase local-media consolidation.

• Newspapers are seeking partnerships with broadband distributors and/or software companies to become the "first screen," or prominent on that screen or portal site, that a consumer uses to navigate online activities.

• Publishers will either compete against themselves and their customers or let other entities do so.

• Newspapers must account for their interactive classified-ad revenues as either newspaper or online revenue, but not both. Their decision could affect whether print or Internet ventures will get the most financial investment in news. This especially concerns media companies with Internet spinoffs.

CHAPTER 3

Market Brand: What's in a Name?

The previous chapter focused on scale and distribution as key elements in media success. But, of course, content does and will matter as well, although "best" is not always synonymous with "most successful." In the modern, fractured marketplace, quality remains important to establish a company's reputation, or brand. For better or worse, a name says it all:

Say *"The New York Times,"* and most news junkies think "gold standard" of journalism.

Say "Newton," and most technology aficionados remember Apple's failed pocket calendars.

A brand name defines a company's quality and success, its method of capturing customers' aspirations and admiration. How that name gains its reputation is often the stuff of myth. By understanding brands, we begin to understand the values driving news company behavior. Toward that end, the *Times*-Newton comparison is instructive.

By most measures, the *Times* represents the best. The *Times* is the largest U.S. daily to publish seven days a week, and it delivers fuller world coverage than its two "larger" rivals, *USA TODAY* and *The Wall Street Journal,* which publish on weekdays only. No other daily devotes more human resources, exceeding 1,150 in news staff worldwide, to covering the events and issues of the day. Even that number is not as spectacular as it seems, and here's why:

By at least one industry benchmark, a well-staffed newspaper employs one editorial staff member per 1,000 subscribers. A 100,000-circulation daily should have a news staff of 100, give or take a few. Indeed, most U.S. dailies come pretty close. By this ratio, the *Times* should have about 1,100 editorial staff members, given its 1.1 million daily circulation (1.8 million on Sunday). Right on the mark.

Is the staff big because the newspaper is? Or is the newspaper big because its staff is? The chicken-and-egg question does not minimize the great coverage, integrity and journalistic leadership forged by the Sulzberger family over the years. And to sell overall staff size as a primary element in brand excellence may not be right, either. To answer our question: In this case, the brand came first: "All the news that's fit to print" was coined a century ago.

Apple's Newton palm-computing device for note-taking and calendars was intended as a breakthrough in the early 1990s. More important to its creators, the Newton would read handwriting and translate it into computer language.

The conventional wisdom is that the Newton failed because it couldn't deliver on that promise. Technology experts disagree. The Newton failed because it had no communications capability, said Peter Schwartz, president of the Global Business Network, a California think tank. Owners would have forgiven the glitches, Schwartz said, if the device had fulfilled a more basic purpose — transmitting messages and meeting dates to other Apple computers. Newton's successors, such as the Palm Pilot, have that capability and are popular with the connected set.

The moral: Internal definitions of success can steer a brand far afield from customers' needs. Fulfilling those needs can trump quality to build brand value, said Adrian Slywotzky of the consulting firm Corporate Decisions Inc. His book, "Value Migration," classifies products according to what customers "care about" and "don't care about." Of Jack Welch's early leadership of General Electric Co., the industrial powerhouse and owner of NBC, Slywotzky writes:

"Welch understood that many of GE's manufactured products had long ago entered the customers' 'I don't care' zone and that customers had too many product options. In contrast, the customer cared deeply about financing. ... The options for meeting this need were fewer."

Welch invested in GE Capital to provide effective financing, making GE a "better" brand because consumers had easier financial access to its products.

Value. Brand. Are these strange concepts for the news business? Isn't publishing truth the ultimate value? Isn't integrity the brand? Yes and no. A brand sets companies and products apart from their competitors, but it isn't enough to simply say, "Our stuff is the best." In what way is it the best?

Most manufacturers have been involved in brand-building for decades. In the 1980s, newspapers began hiring brand managers from consumer-product companies to help boost sales. The practice worked well in advertising departments but mostly failed in marketing and circulation efforts. One reason: The traditional brand manager for packaged goods can change anything and everything about a product to please the consumer, including the packaging and even the ingredients. At newspapers, that role belongs to the editor. Still, brand-building will be key to all news organizations, the responsible person's title notwithstanding.

Six elements are critical in developing news brands for this brave new digital world. Most are common to other industries. A few are unique. Together they will help determine the future of news, one product at a time.

Element No. 1: Filling a need

The first rule of any product, including the news, is to give the consumer something of value — as the user, not the producer, defines value. Would a morning newspaper that only repeats last night's TV news fill a need? Would an evening network newscast that rehashes news from the all-day cable channels? Some successes:

• All-news radio holds its ground despite great media competition because it updates traffic and weather information more often than any other source. It doesn't analyze the test ban treaty. It is utilitarian. People simply want to know how long it will take to get to work or how heavily to bundle their children on a winter day.

• Community newspapers fill a similar niche by publishing local calendars, city council and school board votes, school lunch menus and youth sports scores.

• The most successful Internet Web site for African-Americans is BlackVoices.com, whose slogan is "Where African-Americans Live Online." It attracts more visitors than the popular NetNoir.com ("The Black Network") or other ethnic sites because it allows visitors to post and tell their own stories, creating a virtual community that was needed but didn't previously exist. It has grown to include job recruitment services.

• The Bloomberg and Dow Jones business information services make great sums of money from subscribers who need real-time stock quotes for trading and cannot wait the 15 minutes it takes to get the same information from scores of free Internet information providers.

Pricing is a traditional way to measure public need. If people really want something, they'll pay for it. Yet most newspapers are price sensitive, heavily discounting subscriptions to increase sales volume — a practice called "heroin" by Janet Robinson, general manager of *The New York Times*. Once started, it is almost impossible to stop. On the other hand, business and sports services can increase subscription fees because they deliver reliable, complete, needed data — all the quotes, all the scores, all the players, on the street, on the field, on the court.

At the same time, the pressure to publish free information on the Internet and in print suggests that public attitudes about the value of general day-to-day information has changed. Veronis, Suhler & Associates, an investment bank specializing in media, estimates that 75% of weekly newspaper circulation is free.

Filling needs is imperative but not enough for a news company, or any

> The pressure to publish free information on the Internet and in print suggests that public attitudes about the value of general, day-to-day information have changed.

other, to stand out in a competitive world. Another critical consideration: How is your product different?

Element No. 2: Distinctiveness

At the beginning of any new media era, it's easy to be distinctive. In today's increasingly competitive and fractured media world, it has become very hard. Here are some of the qualities that news-media organizations need to set themselves apart:

• *Talent.* Edward R. Murrow. Walter Cronkite. Huntley and Brinkley. Scotty Reston. Marguerite Higgins. They created strong brands of their own, tied to news operations of their time. TV anchors' salaries today — exceeding $5 million annually for major morning and evening programs — is a modern variant on the value of individual talent as a builder of news brands.

• *Topicality.* Fifteen years ago, public television held the franchise for providing cultural, public interest and children's programming. In a mass-market world, only one such programmer could survive, and only as a nonprofit entity. But in the new fractured and wired world, the Discovery Channel, the History Channel, the Arts & Entertainment Network and the Nickelodeon children's channel all claim pieces of the traditional public-TV audience. Suddenly, PBS offers near-infomercials by financial guru Suze Orman and other popular author-speakers during pledge periods.

• *Timeliness.* Until five years ago, CNN had a lock on up-to-the-minute coverage of global events: the fall of the Berlin Wall; the Gulf War; even the slow-speed chase of O.J. Simpson, which I watched in a London hotel room in 1994. How else would one know what was going on? Today, NBC, Dow Jones, Rupert Murdoch's empire and others challenge that franchise, nationally and internationally. With Princess Diana's death in 1997, CNN lost its No. 1 position in the U.S. to MSNBC and has battled for first place ever since.

In the U.S. homes with cable service, MSNBC is often first with breaking news. When day trader Mark Barton stormed two Atlanta brokerage firms, killing nine people and wounding 13 others — in addition to family members and himself — MSNBC was on the air some 15 minutes before CNN, whose headquarters are in the city where the event took place. CNN executive Eason Jordan scoffs at the notion it is less competitive. "We may get beaten on any given story, but we have an unrivaled group of affiliates at the local level," he said.

A footnote: CNN's "NewsStand" (in partnership with Time Warner sibling Time Inc.) has sought to create a unique news product for CNN and for various magazines. A controversy over accuracy marred its debut, the so-called Operation Tailwind nerve gas story, and both CNN and *Time* magazine retracted the story. Later programs proved to be less sensational and less popular, although its blockbuster "Millennium" series was a hit.

• *Convenience.* Newspapers are mostly local enterprises, but three have succeeded in developing large national circulations. They have several elements in common while serving distinct markets. *USA TODAY* targets weekday business travelers and provides an easy-to-read summary of national events, entertainment, business and comprehensive sports. *The Wall Street Journal* sells to business people generally and provides complete business news, national political coverage, and conservative opinion and commentary. *The New York Times* publishes a comprehensive news, lifestyle and cultural report with a generally liberal editorial page. It is the only one of these "big three" with a Sunday edition. The *Los Angeles Times* tried to enter the national newspaper market, but what niche was left to fill? A take on the nation and world from a California perspective? No one's been able to build a business plan around that idea.

• *Depth.* Among the niche Web sites, The Nando Times has a loyal following of those interested in national and, especially, international news. Nando understands the growing demand for world news, spawned in part by U.S. immigration and global commerce. In August 1999, when a suicide bomber killed a friend of mine in Sri Lanka, Nando delivered a dozen stories, including texts of tributes from President Clinton and U.N. Secretary-General Kofi A. Annan. Finding the articles was simple with a powerful search engine and the "object-oriented, front-end database everyone talks about," said Christian Hendricks, who ran The Nando Times for the McClatchy Co. and is now vice president of McClatchy's Interactive Media.

Hendricks said that by drawing more completely on news sources from around the world, Nando often posts major stories before the AP or Reuters, the major wires serving U.S. newsrooms and Web sites. "Agence France-Presse [and Nando] beat everyone else on Diana," Hendricks said of the British princess's death in a Paris car accident. "CNN doesn't like that. They know what we represent."

• *Exclusivity.* C-SPAN (the Cable-Satellite Public Affairs Network) maintains its unique identity as the only place to see gavel-to-gavel coverage of congressional proceedings, logging 1,000 hours in each chamber per year. At times, the networks and cable channels intrude. During the Clinton impeachment hearings, as many as five different networks carried events live, but when outside the storm of high-profile politics, C-SPAN has the field to itself. A more typical example: In November 1999, EgyptAir Flight 990 crashed within days of two mass killings (one in Honolulu, one in Seattle) as well as President Clinton's veto of the health and labor budget appropriation. CNN and MSNBC carried the veto announcement but immediately returned to live coverage of the crime stories and the crash. Only C-SPAN continued its veto coverage through the subsequent press conference.

C-SPAN offers a good example of brand distinctiveness. Its government coverage draws a loyal following and as many as 30 million viewers a year. Its audience reflects the U.S. population in education, ethnicity and employment, according to founder and CEO Brian Lamb. C-SPAN saw a niche and filled it first.

Element No. 3: Quality

Quality is a key to reputation or brand-building. But measuring news quality across the board can be subjective and situational. Is it better to be first? To be absolutely right? To be totally fair? To provide a different context? What stories do readers and viewers value, and are they the same as journalists' choices? Are they the same for newspapers, radio, television and the Internet? Does a sensational story by definition lack quality?

As news organizations answer these and other questions, they redefine quality within today's multimedia world. Part of the redefinition is a new look at these old standards of journalistic quality:

• *Prizes.* The Pulitzer for newspapers. The Peabody and duPont for radio and television. The Emmys for television. Prizes are one yardstick for news-report quality. The perennial efforts to mount prize-winning series attest to the importance of peer affirmation that journalists seek. In print media, the largest newspapers with the greatest resources tend to win the most prizes. They also tend to develop a "quality" brand. Prizes certainly enhance a brand but cannot overcome basic business problems. *The Oakland Tribune,* during a decade of Maynard family ownership, won more than 150 major journalism prizes, including a Pulitzer. The laurels were no substitute, though, for the absence of a retail base in downtown Oakland.

It's less clear how the public views prizes, but prizes do provide aspirations for news organizations seeking to do good journalism. Hence their proliferation and expansion. This year, for example, the Pulitzer Prize competition accepts online presentations in support of entries in the public service category.

• *Enterprise Reporting.* Among journalists, enterprise reporting is the heart of watchdog journalism. They presume that the public may not know what enterprise reporting is by definition, but the public recognizes it, and values it, when they see it.

This study, from the outset in 1997, identified enterprise news as the single most important standard of quality. It presents new information, not staged events, routine meetings or press releases. It requires enough resources to interest an editor but generally not enough to win a prize (although it could), covering such topics as lending practices, campaign contributions and public contract awards.

The present state of enterprise reporting is unclear. In November 1999, the Project for Excellence in Journalism in Washington, D.C., affiliated with the Columbia University Graduate School of Journalism, cited a decline in enterprise reporting at local TV stations, representing a decline in quality.

One exception is WNBC-TV in New York City, whose news director, Paula Madison, believes in enterprise. She requires each reporter to produce a certain number of original stories — putting "new news" into the global information stream. Understanding her viewers' roots, Madison has sent reporting teams to the Dominican Republic to track down a fugitive murder suspect (the story won a Peabody); to Israel for election coverage; and to Africa to examine game-park practices. This policy, she believes, keeps her station first in news in her market, and the public gets it.

Many journalists argue that the heavy hand of corporate ownership today robs newsrooms of the resources necessary not only for enterprise reporting but for routine coverage of day-to-day events. This issue is real, but despite journalists' protests, it's not entirely clear that the entire news industry is suffering. Some owners have invested massively in expanded local newscasts, cable news and online information. Yet the Project for Excellence claims that expenditures don't equal expansion.

Reliable income and profit figures for broadcasters are closely held and difficult to obtain. Most are estimates cobbled together by investment banking or research firms. Major-market stations are estimated to have pre-tax profit margins of 21%, although it can run as high as 33% for network affiliates, according to Media Dynamics Inc., a research and marketing firm. Small-market stations net an average of 9%. Network owned and operated stations enjoy estimated margins of 45%.

Among the big public media companies, pressures to bolster profits and stock prices often come from founding-family members seeking higher returns from their inheritances. Such was the case among the Binghams of

The Courier-Journal in Louisville, Ky., the Chandlers of Times Mirror Co. and the Bancrofts of Dow Jones & Co. But journalistic lore continues to focus on public ownership as a resource drain.

A typical story: Shortly before he resigned as general manager of *The Dallas Morning News* in 1998, Jeremy Halbreich asked whether a rising profit level, more than 30%, meant it was time to plow more dollars back into the newspaper. He wasn't talking about more coverage per se (which was expanding anyway via a new statewide cable news channel produced in conjunction with the newspaper, its Web site and parent A.H. Belo Corp.'s Texas TV stations). His question was: Do profits beyond a certain point represent underinvestment in the business? Walter Cronkite made a similar point in advocating that media companies aspire, by policy, to the lower returns of bonds rather than the sky-high profits of stocks.

Part of the answer has to do with the company's long-term plans: Is it a cash cow to be milked or is it a field to be planted and replanted? The Daniels family of Raleigh, N.C., solved the problem during its ownership of *The News & Observer* by splitting the baby. "When I took over, the newspaper was making 10% profit," said former owner Frank A. Daniels Jr. "It rose to 22% to 24% as long as business conditions were good. And I kept it there — no higher — choosing to reinvest. For me, it was more a question of whether we were putting enough back in."

• *Profit.* Yes, profit is a benchmark of quality, though a complex one. As media companies invest in new ventures, they usually compete with large dot-com and telecommunications companies with huge capital war chests.

Passionate newspeople love to fight the "bean-counters," but the truth is that certain industry ratios, setting out optimal expenditures for various functions, determine the news report's size and shape in any given year. Although many companies were slow to adopt them, most do so today. The change was especially contentious at large dailies such as *The Philadelphia Inquirer* and the *Los Angeles Times*. These industry benchmarks set standards for more than news operations. Banks, for example, use them to determine interest rates when a company seeks to borrow working capital or funds to grow. Low operating returns result in higher rates.

According to the Inland Cost and Revenue Study, neither newspaper profits nor editorial expenditures have changed much industrywide. In 1980, editorial departments represented about 12.3% of total newspaper expenses. In 1998, the percentage was 12.6%, according to Inland's economic model. Editorial expenditures were somewhat higher at smaller dailies, slightly lower at big ones. As a percentage of income, news expenditures were between 9% and 11% of total revenues. Newspapers' profit margins continue to run under 20%, though many individual papers do much better, said Judy Minson,

Inland's research director.

Good newspaper managers keep news expenses within a sensible range, said John M. Lavine, who heads the Media Management Center at Northwestern University's Medill School of Journalism and Kellogg School of Management. Excluding the big dailies, he said, "A 16% newsroom expenditure may not be great; it may just be sloppy." Excessive investment has a diminishing return.

In the broadcast sector, news investments are increasing along with on-air programming, although station profits generally are down. The National Association of Broadcasters reports that news expenses at network affiliate stations increased from 15% of expenses and 14% of revenues in 1990 to 23% of expenses and 14% of revenues in 1997, the latest NAB figures available. (Among affiliates, revenue appears to be the benchmark for news spending. Independent stations had no news operations in 1990 but are beginning to invest.)

An RTNDA/Ball State University study, published in November 1999, estimates that news programs accounted for 40% of station revenues in 1998, up from 35% two years before. But the number of stations reporting profitable news operations declined to 57% in 1998, from 62% in 1996 — a drop attributed to expansion costs. At the same time, 69% of stations reporting profitable news operations in 1998 said their margins had increased.

"The percentage showing a loss has increased over the same time frame, from 8% to 11%," the researchers' report said. "This may reflect the slow but steady increase in the number of stations starting local news operations. Start-ups generally lose money for at least one or two years. ... The drop in profitability crosses all market sizes except the smallest, with the most pronounced drop in the biggest markets.

"Further, all network affiliates showed drops in profitability except NBC affiliates, which held steady. Fox affiliates dropped the most, perhaps reflecting the greater likelihood of start-up news operations among Fox affiliates. The lower profitability of ABC affiliates (again this year) probably reflects the network's prime-time programming and lead-in weakness."

At CNN and its Headline News channel, "program expenses" have averaged between 17.5% and 20% of revenue over the eight years beginning in 1989, according to the Paul Kagan & Associates media research and consulting company.

So news gathering, while expensive, is a small portion of every medium's operating budget and has been so historically. These expenses have been rising, challenging the notion that record media profits come directly from newsrooms' budgets, although that could be the case at individual properties.

C-SPAN has the easiest approach to it all, supported by cable operators through a self-imposed assessment averaging 5 cents per subscriber per month — or 60 cents a year. Its $33 million budget is enough to fulfill its mission, said CEO Brian Lamb. Even there, with a more narrowly defined mission than that of the commercial media, news telecasting is a fraction of the whole effort, accounting for only 45 of some 260 employees. Producers, program operators, engineers, educators and promotion executives make up the rest of the C-SPAN complement.

Element No. 4: Integrity

Of all the elements of a news organization's reputation, integrity is paramount, and it's under attack on many fronts.

Years of surveys show that the public overwhelmingly believes news coverage serves the purposes of politics or business — not civic interest. Increased public access to primary sources, the raw material of news, seems to increase distrust.

Movies that have popularized journalistic missteps include "The Insider," a recent film about how CBS News' "60 Minutes" killed a whistleblower's story about the tobacco industry's manipulation of nicotine in cigarettes. Many journalists openly questioned whether the impending merger of CBS with Westinghouse Electric Corp. and the fear of a massive lawsuit factored into the network's late-1995 decision.

Journalists continue to question news companies', especially newspapers', many new marketing relationships with business interests. These marketing "synergies," as the corporate types see them, sometimes threaten the newsroom's traditional independence from business operations, from which journalistic credibility flows.

Moreover, journalists in traditional news organizations roundly malign the trend toward Internet publishing (and the attendant fast-forward, 24-hour news cycle) as reducing credibility, even as they rush to join in.

"There's a hunger for integrity," said C-SPAN's Lamb about public aspirations for the news. But what does that mean? Spanning the debate, journalistic integrity has three basic elements: getting it right; staying fair and disentangled from news sources; and taking the high road by pushing issues not for private gain but for the public good.

• *Getting it right.* Legendary columnist Jack Anderson liked to tell a story on himself about the importance of accuracy. Using a researcher's notes, he began a story about power-plant negligence by describing two huge chimneys spewing pollution into the atmosphere. One huge problem: The power plant had three flues, not two. The mistake, Anderson said, robbed the report of any credibility it might have had. People notice.

Theories abound about how accuracy, or lack of it, plays into public support or distrust of traditional news media. News, or any information, is expensive to get at all and more expensive to get right. That's one reason Yellow Page directories are the most profitable publishing enterprise. The cost of getting all those listings correct is prohibitive to all but the established directory publishers, and they guard their franchises jealously, intentionally slipping in mistakes (as Pulitzer and Hearst used to do) to detect copiers.

To many, Internet Webmeister Matt Drudge is the poster boy for all that's wrong with the new cyber-journalism. Drudge claims to pass along what he hears without checking it, amassing a long list of critics who say he confuses the public about the journalistic process. "Rumormonger" is about the nicest characterization of him. Drudge broke the story of how *Newsweek* spiked the Monica Lewinsky story. The essential truth of that report, and its aftermath, sticks in the craw of traditional journalists who verify their stories with multiple sources. Movie-studio executives fume at him, too, because he figures out where they preview feature films and sends his grassroots "reporters" out for unofficial reviews. *Brill's Content* magazine analyzed Drudge's Web site and found it to be about 80% accurate — astoundingly high for someone who never checks a fact.

As news outlets proliferate, so do news critics who monitor accuracy. Some examples:

• CNN dedicates a weekly program, "Reliable Sources," to news-media practices.

• *Brill's Content,* with a reported 225,000 in circulation, began publishing in 1998 as the first step in Steven Brill's for-profit, multimedia plan to promote media accountability. Its ombudsman, retiring Nieman Foundation curator Bill Kovach, in turn criticizes *Content* magazine's criticism.

• The more traditional, university-based journalism reviews have picked up the pace of their own analysis. *Columbia Journalism Review* got David Laventhol to sign on as publisher and editorial director. The retired Times Mirror editor-at-large is an industry leader with a strong reputation for integrity from both the editorial and business sides.

• In 1999, New York City-based radio host Don Imus joined the effort part-time, inviting listeners to phone in items from *The New York Times* that breach the newspaper's newly published guide to style and usage.

Every year brings celebrated cases of getting it wrong, even among the best. The *San Jose* (Calif.) *Mercury News* had to retract a story implicating the Central Intelligence Agency in urban drug trafficking. Under the new pressures of the 24-hour news cycle, *The Dallas Morning News* retracted a story (published only on its Web site) claiming that a White House steward witnessed President Clinton and Monica Lewinsky in intimate encounters.

Whether the public pays attention to these mistakes is unclear. Do they amount to trends in the public mind, like school shootings? What role does our journalistic handwringing play? Television, locally and nationally, beats newspapers in public credibility polls. Does the public's ability to see and hear sources directly on the air contribute to that assessment?

A more basic issue is the knowledge gap between the public and journalists on any number of subjects. As the world becomes more complex, reporters have less opportunity to build specific knowledge of any one subject. Journalists' common-sense standard is a moving target. Covering a fire on Main Street is one thing. Examining municipal contract-letting may prove something else again. Finance, engineering, land use and the like are specialized subjects that most reporters know superficially. On the other hand, the public is an amalgam of individuals with specific knowledge and, as in Jack Anderson's smokestack example, calibrates its reliance on news with personal knowledge.

Understanding journalistic vulnerability on this point, some organizations support reporting with just-in-time information about stories. The Los Angeles-based Foundation for American Communications, for example, provides lists of specialists who help journalists decipher complex issues. The Internet is a boon too. Have a question on a story? Log on to search for the answer. It's a beginning, but it doesn't fully bridge the knowledge gap between reporters and the public on too many issues.

• *Freedom from entanglements.* Integrity also hinges on a news organization's struggle for independence, a time-worn fight. Most U.S. newspapers began as extensions of political parties. The First Amendment was more concerned with ensuring free opinion than factual reporting. Many newspaper names reflect this history, such as the *Arkansas Democrat-Gazette* of Little Rock and the *Press-Republican* of Plattsburgh, N.Y.

Yet a funny thing happened on the way to the Industrial Revolution: News evolved. The telegraph age encouraged short sentences, just the facts, de-emphasizing the focus on opinion. News companies became family-owned, and many publishers shifted their allegiances from political networks to their communities' business networks. The merchant went to the bank to finance shipments of merchandise and newspaper advertising to move that merchandise. The ads ran, the goods sold, the bank was repaid, and the cycle repeated itself.

In colonial times, politically strong printers could resist government pressure. Later, financially strong publishers could resist advertising pressure — yet persist it did. Here's a modern version of the conflict: A.H. Belo Corp.'s 1999 investment in the Dallas Mavericks basketball team. Reporters at the *Morning News* objected. How, they asked, can we fairly report on our own team? The same question has been asked in Chicago, Los Angeles, Phoenix and in other cities where newspapers or television stations invest in sports teams.

Even more discussed was the controversy at the *Los Angeles Times* over the

Journalists continue to question news companies', especially newspapers', many new marketing relationships with business interests. These marketing "synergies," as the corporate types see them, sometimes threaten the newsroom's traditional independence from business operations.

proper distance between the news and business operations. In November 1999, the *Times* staff erupted in near mutiny when it became known that a *Times* magazine edition devoted to the new Staples Center sports arena had been published under an arrangement in which the newspaper and the arena split ad revenues 50-50. *The New York Times* broke the story in the mainstream press, only to report quietly a few days later that *The Boston Globe,* which it owns, engaged in a similar practice in 1995.

Journalists believe the public values a news organization that is both independent and local. In the context of branding and news quality, it means journalists may need to redefine independence. The paradox: The public seems to want both arm's-length reporting and coverage tethered to town interests.

Journalistic objectivity traditionally means that reporting is impersonal, drawn mechanically from facts thought to be true, in the same way a topographical map reports a landscape. Tort and criminal law, however, set a common-sense standard for objectivity: what a reasonable person would do or construe, given certain facts. This assessment is based on common values and fairness, not a topographical map but an impressionistic portrayal of the landscape. Increasingly, the public perceives journalistic standards of objectivity as pseudo-scientific and disembodied, and journalists are losing public support.

This changing perception of what journalists should be — from aloof observers to fair-minded citizens — produced important reporting at two newspapers in 1996.

Two highly profitable U.S. dailies, *The News & Observer* in Raleigh, N.C., and *The Orange County* (Calif.) *Register,* won Pulitzer prizes that year — on hog farming and fertility clinics, respectively. As it happened, both had been involved in corporate strategy sessions in the months before their prize-winning efforts began. Both also employed the same consultant, Synectics Inc. of Cambridge, Mass., to help form those strategies. In each case, said Synectics' then-President William Boggs, the organizations defined their newspapers as more than truth-tellers or reporters of information. Each of the newspapers' plans called for operating as a local citizen, with a stake in their communities' wealth and well-being. *Register* Publisher N. Christian Anderson III was fiercely combative on that point as he described the *Register*'s ongoing circulation battle with the *Los Angeles Times*:

"No one else cares about Orange County the way we do. No one else lives here every day," he said. On a major story, community sources "call us first." That's just how the *Register* got information for its Pulitzer-winning series about abuses at a local fertility clinic in a renowned medical center.

As many news organizations foster public perceptions of journalists as fair-minded community citizens, they tread a thin line — home-grown truth being seen as healthier, more organic, yet still at risk of contamination.

• *Taking a stand.* Heroics are the stuff of news brands: the showdown with power; the reporter packed off to jail to honor confidentiality; the David-vs.-Goliath refusal to let government intrude on the journalistic process.

Did CBS' refusal to air the 1995 report on the Brown & Williamson Tobacco Corp. harm its name and brand with the public as well as the press? Many argued it did. Was the decision of the same mindset that has kept CBS News in the No. 3 spot for years?

If a bad stand damages a news organization's brand name, can a good one enhance it? At *The Oakland Tribune,* for example, the Maynard family decided that we could no longer accept handgun advertising. Hawking assault guns on the sports page seemed crazy, given the local murder rate and our editorial positions against violence and for gun control. The policy change brought praise from community leaders. And economic pain. The newspaper sacrificed some $100,000 in revenue. Was it worth it? Yes. Could we ever calculate how many Oakland subscribers we gained or retained because of it? No.

On the national stage, the two biggest reputation-boosting stories of the last 30 years were the Pentagon Papers and Watergate. *The New York Times* and *The Washington Post* were focal points of the Pentagon Papers drama. The *Post* took the lead on Watergate. These cases are related, illustrating that doing the right thing isn't always obvious at first.

The New York Times spent what now would be more than $1 million in legal fees to defend its right to expose the Johnson administration's lies about the progress of the Vietnam War. Within the *Times,* it was a secret operation. A whole group of reporters and editors disappeared from the newsroom and moved to a nearby hotel to read documents and produce their stories.

Peter Millones, who ran business operations for the *Times* newsroom then, said he asked the paper's finance officer to deposit $50,000 in a special account for a special project. To his own surprise, he got it. The sum would be equivalent to several hundred thousand dollars today. Would any executive make that kind of blind withdrawal today?

The *Times* understood the story's importance, occurring at the height of the anti-war movement, and was willing to risk everything for it. The *Post* got the papers later. When the government threatened to restrain the *Times* from publishing additional installments, the *Post* agreed to do so.

All great dramas have subplots — in this case two, one for each paper. For the *Times,* it was the Nixon administration's attempt to subpoena the notes of reporter Earl Caldwell, who covered the Black Panther Party in California, the same year as the Pentagon Papers case. For the *Post,* it was the same administration's challenge to the Post Co.'s broadcast-license renewal in retaliation for publishing the Pentagon Papers.

The *Times* did not see the administration's challenges to journalistic independence as related and ordered Caldwell to produce his notes and testify. The New York Black Journalists Association found a constitutional lawyer, Anthony Amsterdam of Stanford University, to represent him separately from the *Times* and pro bono. Ultimately, the U.S. Supreme Court rejected Caldwell's argument, but its opinion led to press shield laws nationwide. Later, the *Times* supported reporters thus challenged, and its reputation as a defender of press freedoms continued to grow.

Donald E. Graham, now *Post* publisher and chairman and CEO of The Washington Post Co., recalled the Pentagon Papers case as a critical influence on its Watergate coverage. The heavy-handed challenge to the Post Co.'s broadcast licenses, he said, made his institution readier to believe the reporting of Bob Woodward and Carl Bernstein, which came under great criticism for nearly two years. Few believed a sitting president would countenance, let alone lead, an organized campaign of spying and sabotage against political foes. The *Post* knew better.

While the coverage depressed the Post Co.'s stock price, the stakes were higher than that. At issue was the newspaper's ability to conduct business without government control or seizure. In short, Watergate represented more than just a good story.

In the intervening years, both dailies have had incidents that either burnished or blemished their brand names. But on balance, they still win the reputational war in the industry and the marketplace. How much have their good names been worth in drawing outstanding journalists, raking in awards, avoiding further showdowns and garnering ad dollars? Uncounted, uncountable millions.

Local civic-journalism efforts can be equally important. In 1998, *The Seattle Times* launched a campaign to defeat Initiative 200, which would dismantle affirmative-action efforts. The campaign went beyond an editorial page crusade. It included advertising against the measure, which raised newsroom concerns about editorial independence. Despite the *Times'* objections, the measure passed — but not in Seattle, Publisher Frank A. Blethen noted.

The *Akron Beacon Journal* won the 1994 Pulitzer Gold Medal for Public Service for a series on race relations and associated community-building programs. The effort made Akron a stop for President Clinton as he rolled out his initiative on race.

Independent producers won a 1998 Peabody Award for their public-television documentary, "Travis," the story of a boy with AIDS whose grandmother rallied a San Francisco community to his care.

Courageous news organizations can build a brand with integrity. But without a long-term institutional commitment, they might not be able to sustain it.

Element No. 5: Advertising and Marketing

It's ironic but not surprising that news organizations make most of their money from advertising but rarely advertise themselves. There's a reason: It's expensive. But news organizations that ignore advertising do so at their peril.

Internet companies are the biggest new advertisers in traditional media. They spent an estimated $1 billion in 1999 on TV spots alone, vying for dot-com name recognition and market share in the online-shopping arena. Traditional media may be losing audience, but they still drive business.

As dot-com advertising proliferated during the 1999 holiday season, former *New York Times* executive editor Max Frankel noted in the *Times'* Sunday magazine, "Quite remarkably, it seems the New Media have suddenly decided to enrich the Old. Or, if you prefer irony in your paradox, the Old Media are greedily wolfing down the poison that will hasten their destruction by the New."

Over the years, as news industry groups sought to bolster their own businesses, advertising became key. The Newspaper Association of America, for example, developed a high-profile print and broadcast ad campaign, featuring celebrities and other public figures, to encourage newspaper reading. After Mel Karmazin took control of CBS in 1997, he took the "CBS Evening News" from third place to nearly first by promoting it during unsold advertising slots on the company's radio network. Media analysts, not understanding the mechanics, saw CBS' rise as a victory of "substance" over "fluff." Actually, it was ads over news. NBC, too, is promoting its new Internet portal, Snap.com, on its television and cable broadcasts. It's got a lot riding on Snap.com's success as the centerpiece of the network's new publicly traded company, NBC Internet Inc. (NBCi). ABC promotes Go.com, in which it has invested and for which it provides news and entertainment content.

In the crowded mixed-media world, advertising and promotion will become even more important to mature news products that want to enhance their brands and visibility. It could get rough: CNN has already rejected an ad for the Internet magazine, Salon, deciding that the revenue was not worth building brand awareness for a jaunty competitor.

Element No. 6: Diversity

Staff and coverage diversity can be important to any mass-audience news operation's claim of integrity. Columnist and editor Les Payne of *Newsday* in Long Island, N.Y., is fond of describing the world as "a colored shirt with a few white buttons." For now, the U.S. is a button, but demographic trends predict that by mid-century, the U.S. will be the shirt, as most residents will be people of color.

Media companies have struggled to make staffs and coverage representative of their communities for more than 30 years. The 1968 Kerner Commission Report found the news media "shockingly backward" in hiring and covering minorities. Progress has been slow, and the rate of America's population diversification is accelerating.

As if population changes aren't challenging enough, proliferating competition looms large in the form of niche weeklies, magazines, narrow-casted radio and television. Daily newspapers and network TV programs that disregard the impact of diversity put themselves at risk, giving up a chance to expand their otherwise shrinking audiences. Local television has already figured this out.

One of the big stories of economic expansion in the 1990s is the growth of the minority middle class, which often finds coverage of its communities to be "lite" or just plain wrong. For them, niche Internet communities provide a growing alternative.

Additionally, immigration and the rise of ethnic print and broadcast media will truly challenge news purveyors, especially in large cities. Underscoring this success are some urban newspapers' efforts to grow circulation through partnerships with ethnic papers that will carry the metro daily inside. Maria Elena Salinas of the Spanish-language network Univision has an audience as large as ABC's Peter Jennings.

Whether, and how, news media will cover the changing population will be important to brand-building in the digital world. Responsive coverage will drive readership and viewership to some extent. It certainly will affect societal attitudes about diversity. Demographic trends suggest that immigrants and the young (with more people of color than in the older U.S. age brackets) will be key to market success. Few news organizations, however, have strategies equal to this dynamic force, much less a relevant brand slogan to sell to the public.

Niche Magazines Fill Information Voids

Traditional news media compete with numerous niche magazines for consumers' attention and loyalty. Among the most successful has been *Essence*, a 30-year-old lifestyle magazine for African-American women, with 1 million sales monthly. Like *Ebony* magazine before it, *Essence* filled an information void left by daily media, which did not appreciate the importance of covering the growing middle-class minority market. They do now. "Diversity" has become a key ingredient of media marketing strategies as well as news coverage.

Meantime, Essence Communications Inc. CEO Edward T. Lewis has diversified his holdings to include *Essence for Men; Latina,* a new bilingual magazine for Hispanic women; book publishing; product licensing; arts and cultural-event sponsorship; and television production. He has built a brand with a reputation for hipness and authenticity.

Essence Editorial Director Susan L. Taylor sold 400,000 copies of her book of inspirational writings through advertising in her magazine and through a network of social groups and churches. It was never listed as a best seller, as such sales were not captured by the traditional distribution measurements. But the relationships are being formed at a time when customer loyalty is bankable. And Lewis is seeking to realize the value by offering his company for merger or sale.

CHAPTER 4

Generation Gap: The Soft Underbelly of Change

I n the rankings of top 20th-century news coverage, few stories rate higher than Edward R. Murrow's 1940 CBS radio reports of the bombing of London. Media historians also highly rank Bob Woodward and Carl Bernstein's early-1970s Watergate coverage for *The Washington Post* and free-lance reporter Seymour Hersh's 1970 dispatches documenting U.S. military atrocities at My Lai in Vietnam. Each story carried great historic importance. And each came from brash young reporters, underscore young: Murrow was 31, the senior member of the "Murrow boys" who built up CBS News in the 1950s; Woodward and Bernstein were in their late 20s, Hersh in his early 30s.

Ever since Ben Franklin apprenticed as a teen-age printer, the news business in America has been the province of energetic young journalists, supervised and sometimes reined in by gruff, jaded elders. But a funny thing happened on the way to the information age — at least in the traditional media. The gray-haired set has captured the news business. This generational domination is far more complete than racial or even gender gaps, more technology-sensitive, and a major factor in young adults' news consumption patterns.

The proportion of professional daily newspaper staff members younger than 25 dropped from 10% in 1988 to 3% in 1998. The youth census is better in television news, yet many anchors at large urban stations have kept those seats for 20 years or more. The best example may be the staff of "60 Minutes," the most highly rated TV news program of the 20th century, whose correspondents range in age from the mid-50s to low 80s.

Why the changed staffing patterns? Among the many reasons:

• Reporters are better educated and entering the job market later in life.

• A news career is less attractive for bright young people when traditional media jobs offer low starting salaries but Internet businesses offer big salaries and other incentives.

• The modern two-career family makes it more difficult for people to move, keeping incumbents in jobs longer.

• Baby boomers, now entering their 40s and 50s, constitute a gigantic population lump in newsrooms.

Whatever the causes, the effect is critical for the future of news. Reader and viewership numbers say young people do not engage traditional news media in the numbers of their parents or even their older siblings. These patterns will not change with maturity. Research and experience show that over the past two decades, consumption of traditional news media has not increased as young adults have aged. "Generational replacement" is a dead concept for daily newspapers and network television.

Some news organizations have recognized the disparity and tried to remedy it. They failed. They've mostly given up trying to figure it out — at least in traditional media. Instead, they came up with token offerings to the young: a few columnists; a weekly entertainment section delivered separately; a Web site tethered to the media mothership.

For all their technology, knowledge of the news and knowledge of youthful news usage, mature media have created few new ways to engage young adults in public-affairs information. Only magazines (e.g., *Teen People, Sports Illustrated for Kids*) and a few of the newer, larger online organizations are tapping into this emerging market.

What does the generation gap mean for the future size of news-media audiences? What does it mean for civic knowledge? Is there a connection between the graying of the traditional newsroom and the diminishing appeal of news to the young? Who are the Ed Murrows of the digital age?

Steve Case probably fits the bill best. He helped create America Online, the largest distributor of Internet news, while he was still in his late 20s. At 32, he became its CEO. Now he is poised to head AOL Time Warner, a merger announced in January 2000. Though not a journalist, he understands the role of news in his online community — and uses traditional news sources as part of his strategy. As a consequence, AOL boasts 10 times more subscribers than the largest U.S. daily newspaper, and the AOL brand is becoming more trusted as a news source than the much older TV networks.

"People now turn to the Net on a story to find out what's happening and then to talk about it," he said. "Users mourned [Princess] Diana's death online. They were able to connect and share an experience — not just become informed. ... TV can speak to you but cannot reason. It can provoke response but cannot hear it."

Case's sensibility resonates with young adults, but it is one that few middle-age news executives appear to understand or value.

Digitization revisited: How big a gap?

The news business has watched its audience age since the dawn of television. A publisher of the now-defunct *Washington Star* was known to quip, each time he saw a hearse, "There goes another of my readers."

He was referring to the almost linear relationship between news habits and age: Older people consume more of everything the news media offer, especially policy reporting, and younger people consume the least of all, except for entertainment and sports news. The Radio and Television News Directors Foundation documented these differences in a 1997 report, "Generation X and the News," finding that:

• Viewers of network evening newscasts and Sunday morning talkfests have an average age approaching 60.

• Those older than 50 watch network news an average of 3.2 days a week, compared with 1.9 days for those younger than 30.

• Less than 30% of adults under 25 said they "read a newspaper yesterday," compared with nearly 70% of people over 50.

• Those born after 1964 have had significantly different life experiences shaping their media habits. And their increasingly productive, fast and mobile lifestyles, involving more single-parent households or families where both parents work, allow less familial time at home to pass on traditional news habits.

In a nation whose median age is 35.5, virtually every study of TV news use across generations shows the same pattern of older viewership. Ken Auletta, who wrote about media in *The New Yorker* for years, likes to joke, "You can tell who's watching television news by the ads: laxatives, denture creams" and, more recently, Viagra.

Beginning in the late 1970s, newspaper editors' and publishers' associations worked jointly on readership studies, trying to rebuild lagging circulation, especially among young adults. A key assumption was that news consumption was age-related behavior. Historically, as people "matured," bought houses, had families and settled into communities, they read newspapers and watched the evening news in larger numbers. Veronis, Suhler & Associates' 1999 Communications Industry Report still predicts that newspaper circulation will grow slightly in the next few years because the over-50 population will swell as baby boomers age. At some point, though, the generational shift is likely to hit — and hit hard.

Despite all their research and trial-and-error efforts, daily newspapers are simply not prepared. The late James K. Batten, who was CEO of Knight Ridder, spent a great deal of time and money probing age-related media behavior. What would he do if the presumption that age enhances media use proved wrong? "I don't want to even think about it," he once said, tongue in cheek. Unfortunately, the assumption is proving to be wrong. Young people who did not grow up reading newspapers tend not to do so later. They simply have too many other choices — some of them, like the World Wide Web, unimagined in the 1970s when such assumptions were made.

RTNDF has documented a generation of adults who never adopted the habit of watching evening news. Why should they? In many ways, it's an artifact from a time when families looked and behaved quite differently. So network-news audiences, already down to one-third of the adult population, may decline further.

Today's digitized, fractured, refrigerated news-media world appeals to younger people who have grown up comfortable with computers and technology. They get their news when they want it and how they want it — weekly, on cable, by satellite or online.

In contrast, many of those preparing the news shy away from today's tools and rules. Some are outright technophobes. More than a few prominent journalists don't use the Internet. Many senior editors who criticize controversial Webmaster Matt Drudge have never visited his Web site, which is mostly an entertaining portal that links users to a variety of media.

Journalists with these sensibilities don't connect with the young, and neither does their coverage. Some news executives are beginning to understand this. As they do, in the finite world of print, they unceremoniously ax the old warhorses to make way for something new. In 1999, *The New York Times* fired from its op-ed page both humorist Russell Baker and former executive editor Abe Rosenthal. They were replaced by clever baby boomers — a bow to the middle generation yet symbolizing the continuing generation gap with younger people.

How costly a gap?

As true mass audiences became more difficult to assemble, media began to focus on "mini-masses." Advertisers value these subgroups according to their buying habits, demographic groupings and sometimes location.

While older people have most of the money and spend a lot of it, mass-media advertising influences them the least. A number of high-end or specialty magazines cater to their tastes. The young women who control the family purse are the biggest target for mass media, so advertisers pay a premium to get their attention.

NBC Executive Vice President Edward L. Scanlon underscores the importance of demographics to TV-news economics by comparing the advertising rates for CBS' "60 Minutes" and NBC's Sunday "Dateline." More than 30 years old, "60 Minutes" is the original and most respected network news-magazine. It consistently ranks among the top 10 programs in weekly prime-

> **Reader and viewership numbers say young people do not engage traditional news media in the numbers of their parents or even their older siblings. These patterns will not change with maturity. ... "Generational replacement" is a dead concept for daily newspapers and network television.**

time ratings. But the average age of that audience is close to 60, so it cannot command the same premium as "Dateline," with its younger, predominantly female viewers.

"Dateline" has one-third the viewership of "60 Minutes" yet commands more per unit of sale, said NBC's Scanlon. The bottom line: Younger viewers are worth more to advertisers.

NBC has been criticized for the story selection that produces such different demographic results. Media critics (frequently older and male) accuse the program of having no edge, of running soft features, of pandering to women. They criticize the "NBC Nightly News" the most. Historically, the networks' evening news was a mountaintop review of politics and policy, with a few national trends and scientific and medical breakthroughs thrown in. Many argue that cable news and the Internet rendered this old formula obsolete. We don't need to tune in to the news to see Congress. It's on C-SPAN all day. We don't need to watch tonight to see those pictures from Mars. We can download them from the NASA site. Still, those who grew up with the formula revere it. Network newscasts, they contend, are for the most important, heavy-duty stories of the day. Period.

"Nightly News" anchor Tom Brokaw frames the criticism in terms of news providers' struggle to accommodate demographic changes by age and gender.

"What's soft and what's hard news anymore?" he asked. "If a gavel fell in Washington, would that be 'hard'? If a woman goes home from work and joins an online support group, is that 'hard' or 'soft'? It's truly an important story of our time — women moving in and out of the workplace.

"We've been accused of pandering to women, who have always been more important in our audience. Was all that political coverage pandering to politicians?"

He said NBC organizes its evening broadcast each day around four segments, treated as a hierarchy that begins with traditional big-newsmaker stories but adds ones that "capture the changing values in American life." The mix of policy and lifestyle coverage has proved a bankable strategy. NBC commands higher ad rates as well as ratings and a more desirable audience demographically.

Sports draws the young men, and networks have adopted different strategies to capture this segment. Broadcast rights to professional events have become so expensive that networks weigh their choices carefully. ABC and CBS spent huge amounts for NFL football rights. CBS beat out ESPN for some college football games. Fox, an early big spender for sports programming, has developed regional sports networks. NBC, more focused on women, opted out of football, broadcasting instead the Olympics and professional basketball, including women's games.

We can't precisely calculate the generation gap's cost to news operations, but traditional media companies clearly are losing younger audiences. Organizations like AOL and MTV, which grab youthful eyes, deliver news within their own frameworks.

News industry gap-filling

So far, traditional news organizations have managed the generation gap around the edges. No big effort has taken hold.

In the 1980s, Knight Ridder researched baby boomers through its "34-45" project, named for the age range it was targeting. The results led to various news-packaging innovations at the Boca Raton, Fla., newspaper it owned at the time, *The News*. The whole industry awaited the loud "a-ha," signaling that they had found the information lariat to rope in this wayward generation.

It never came. Years later, author and Oxygen Media correspondent Farai Chideya sought the reasons for Gen-Xers' differential news-media patterns during her fellowship at The Freedom Forum Media Studies Center in New York City. Her survey research and content analysis failed to nail down an overarching theory, but she found at least one clue to the gap. Chideya, a Gen-Xer herself, showed that the news rarely quotes young people as sources — even in stories about issues affecting their lives. The health insurance debate, for example, is probably of greatest interest to the youngest workers, whose frequent employment as permanent "temps" often denies them coverage. Many stories about health insurance quote politicians but not the uninsured. Their voices are muted in news — a variant on AOL CEO Steve Case's observation that mainstream news media can invoke a response with its stories but can't "hear" that response.

Few audiences are more civic-minded or mature than public-television viewers. The Public Broadcasting Service, like most media operations, sought to close its generation gap a few years ago with programming for teen-agers.

The effort bombed. Executives felt they were "pandering" to an audience with no real interest in PBS, possibly alienating loyal supporters in the process.

Some new ventures designed and produced by and for the young have worked by offering "old" news in new ways — interactively; tight and bright, as at *USA TODAY;* and surrounded by the greatest youth attraction, music, as at MTV. Here are some snapshots of those two success stories.

In 1980 the Gannett Co. (by then the largest newspaper company in the United States) corralled four executives, ages 29 to 31, to work on Project NN (for Nation's Newspaper). The "Young Geniuses," as they were called, set out to study the feasibility of a new national newspaper. Two years later, their efforts resulted in the launch of *USA TODAY,* now the nation's largest circulating daily. Publisher Thomas Curley was one of the four young executives who planned its creation.

Then-Gannett CEO Allen H. Neuharth, who often bragged about his planning team's youth, realized that success would hinge on designing a newspaper for a generation of adults who grew up on quick-delivery TV news.

"The reason newspaper circulation was sliding was because they were not very interesting to the TV generation, who would not fight their way through a dull, gray newspaper," Neuharth said. He knew that young adults' approach to news and information differed from his own. Neuharth had the vision, but he depended on the Young Geniuses to help interpret that vision for the target audience. He ensconced the group near his home in Cocoa Beach, Fla., under older-generation supervision, and charged it with determining how to produce, distribute and sell a unique news product to readers and advertisers. A mixed group of Gannett executives and journalists further developed the concept to draw the target audience.

With its launch in 1982, *USA TODAY* fulfilled its generational promise. Printed with the bright graphics of color television, it sold from newsracks resembling TV sets. Its short stories and blanket coverage of entertainment and sports appealed especially to the young. Established journalists despised it. They called *USA TODAY* "McPaper" for its bite-size news items — informational fast food. One joker suggested that *USA TODAY* would require the creation of a new journalistic prize: best investigative paragraph.

Yet its modern mix of generational, geographic and culturally diverse coverage was popular both with young people and other former newspaper nonreaders. *USA TODAY's* success launched a debate about its perceived lack of substantive content. In the two decades since, "McPaper" has matured along with its target audience, running more investigative and longer stories while remaining popular with youthful readers.

Like its print ancestor *Rolling Stone* magazine, MTV captures young people where they live — with their music — and pulls them into a multimedia experience that includes the news on its cable channel, amid the music videos and celebrity profiles, as well as on its Web site. MTV does not present news the way middle-age adults recognize it. After all, it was an MTV reporter who asked President Clinton, "Boxers or briefs?" When the president admitted to lying about his relationship with Monica Lewinsky, MTV News presented the story in the voice of its constituents, with the lead-in, "Pearl Jam and Ol' Dirty, other musicians, react to Clinton address." Among this group of performers, at least, the president's privacy had been violated unfairly.

MTV sometimes weaves news tightly into music and lifestyle offerings. In election coverage, for example, the news is intertwined with music programming. "You can't separate them," said Farai Chideya, who worked for MTV News during the 1996 presidential election.

Stopping youth violence is a crusade. Any adults surprised by the school shootings around the country in recent years would have been less so had they tuned into MTV News. The problem was long discussed in programs and on its Web sites. MTV's year-long campaign, "Fight for Your Rights," debunks the idea that youth violence is the sole province of poor, inner-city communities. Mainstream media, awash in coverage of street crime, politics and celebrity, have not hit upon the real problem of violence in the lives of America's young adults. MTV has.

MTV documentaries also address youth violence. Among them, an updated version of "Scared Straight" followed youthful offenders on a trip to a maximum-security prison to show them what their lives could be like if they don't straighten up. MTV held a contest to create the best anti-violence public-service announcement around the theme, "Speak Your Peace." MTV also hosts Web-site discussions and local activities related to youth violence.

Civics 101: Who's missing the point?

Media surveys of youth civic knowledge ask questions about government and current affairs. "Who's the Speaker of the House?" is a favorite — although in 1999 one needed a scorecard to follow the bouncing gavel from Newt Gingrich to Robert Livingston to Dennis Hastert.

Such surveys find youthful knowledge wanting and conclude that young people just don't read anymore. But media-usage patterns don't bear that out: Young people do read, just not daily newspapers. They read alternative weeklies, magazines, Sunday newspapers, books and online information. The generation gap seems to prevent baby-boomer newsroom leaders from understanding that.

Traditional dailies unintentionally lost youth readers by their own practices. They stopped using kids to deliver newspapers, an activity that bound young people to the news business and the news. They didn't sufficiently push Newspaper in Education programs, although a collegiate program at Penn State University has shown promise. Free copies of several newspapers are delivered to dormitories each morning. Over the fall, newspaper reading rose on campus. As a result of the program's apparent success, the Audit Bureau of Circulations ruled that newspapers can count such free distribution in their sales totals. With that change, newspapers around the country have started emulating the program on other campuses.

Worst of all, U.S. newspapers abandoned high schools. "Death by Cheeseburger," a Freedom Forum study by Judith D. Hines, documented the decline of vigorous high school journalism. Relationships between school administrators and student reporters can be contentious at best because the issues can be raw (drugs, abortion, weapons, depression, gang behavior) and the language foul. Faculty members are reluctant to supervise such risky enterprises. Entire generations grow up now without understanding the vital role of an unfettered media in a democracy. As a result, high school student surveys show that most think school newspapers should not publish vote counts in student elections to avoid embarrassing the losers. It's another chicken-and-egg problem: Have young people abandoned traditional media, or have traditional media abandoned young people?

Some attempts to cover youthful issues outside the schools include a student news service, Children's Express. Most notably, the Pacific News Service in San Francisco publishes a weekly newspaper, Yo, written by and for teenagers throughout the Bay Area. Public television produces and broadcasts POV (for Point of View), a series which includes documentaries about some of the grittier issues of the life of young people. Coincidentally, Freedom Communications Inc. has developed a slick monthly magazine for young men, which it also calls POV. Nickelodeon carries important youth news programs. Channel One distributes TV news daily to high schools nationwide.

Voice and perception

No one doubts that each generation finds a voice in its popular music. The Woodstock festival was a defining event for the 1960s protest movement, but New York Times editors did not understand that and almost didn't staff it. They sent one of their young reporters.

Entertainment, including sports, is a leading intergenerational organizing format. But what about news? Is there such a thing as an authentic generational voice for news? Can traditional news organizations harness it? In a fractured media world, does it matter?

Omar Wasow is a Gen-X Internet entrepreneur and commentator for NBC and MSNBC. As he explained the news-media generation gap, "Traditional media [have] a hard time understanding that we are not just passive recipients

> **Those who came of age before television believe that narrative flow is the only way to integrate knowledge and language. ... Interactive media, however, are giving rise to new perceptual styles. The visual acuity used to navigate today's multimedia world is astounding.**

of information. We are active participants. We watch television but less of it. Video games and hip-hop have made us receivers and creators, all at once."

Nancy Peretsman, an investment banker at Allen and Co., which backed the Purple Moon Web site for young girls, said, "Every Saturday morning there were 500,000 girls who were not watching television but were e-mailing each other, talking to each other." That was before financial troubles forced the site to scale back its operations.

Wasow also spoke of the different perceptions between news producers and their would-be young consumers. "Younger people are suspicious of traditional media's sense of authority," he said. "We really think of our voices as different from the voices of authority. They always have to be right, always have to control the conversation.

"The journalistic ethic aspires to be objective, but it fails often enough to make young people suspicious of the news. It's an integrity issue. Traditional news media have very little integrity with young people." To get it, Wasow said, "They must be more honest about their failures."

Much has been written about the Gen-Xers' characteristics but little of this writing has been by Gen-Xers in traditional publications. Therefore, little of the coverage has the respect of Gen-X, and if one characteristic can motivate this age group, it is respect. Adults don't command authority, they must earn it.

Since young people see "adult" news outlets as disrespectful, they don't engage them regularly. In two years of research, this study found no basic awareness of this generational attitude among news or marketing executives.

Prime-time entertainment series, which need young viewers to command higher advertising rates, are figuring this out, though. The Fox channel was first. "The Simpsons" captured a generation, if cynically. Fox has tapped into the generational vibe again, designing its news-program screen with numerous related-but-different elements, working away from the linear, one-thing-at-a-time information design, said New York University media historian Mitchell Stephens. For example, on-screen text may add information to a story being told on the air. This is an incremental step toward reaching the young, who are very quick, very busy and possess greater visual literacy than boomers themselves can muster, Stephens said.

The basic differences between each generation's learning styles may well be the major problem impeding new product design in traditional media. Those who came of age before television believe that narrative flow is the only way to integrate knowledge and language. They are fierce newspaper readers. Television and radio use one-way narrative, too, though sped up. Interactive media, however, are giving rise to new perceptual styles. The visual acuity used to navigate today's multimedia world is astounding. One standup comic quipped, "My kids can click on a channel, figure out what's on and reject it before I can even see an image."

In his book, "The Rise of the Image, the Fall of the Word," media historian Stephens argues that media are in a major transition, from language to moving image as the defining form of knowledge transfer.

"Print reinforces a certain kind of logic: one-thing-at-a-time, one-thing-leads-directly-to-another logic, if/then, cause/effect — the logic most of us have internalized," he writes. That is not the logic of fast-paced moving video, he contends, and the young have more experience with doing more than one thing at a time, called "multitasking." Young people can listen to music or watch television while doing homework. Recent surveys show that half of all computer users watch television at the same time. In the world of linear perception, such behavior is heresy, yet it is real and getting more so for the young.

What traditional informational products are being designed around these new patterns of perception? Not many. Internet browser design (pioneered at the National Center for Advanced Supercomputing at the University of Illinois at Urbana-Champaign) is the province of digital companies, not news organizations.

What research exists tends to be product-oriented or incremental: goggles for virtual reality; enhancements of live video to Web sites; better data compression; electronic paper; "wearables," i.e., garments with microprocessing and communications wiring woven into the fabric. But where is the gene-splitting, silicon-chip breakthrough in understanding storytelling or information architecture?

"Interactive Cinema" is one interesting project being developed by Glorianna Davenport at the Massachusetts Institute of Technology. It is a form of interactive TV documentary that allows the viewer to pick and choose elements of the story. Graphic elements on the screen guide understanding. For example, captions identifying the speakers might change color, depending on whether they support or oppose the issue being discussed. Video-game players would easily recognize these visual cues. The ability to use such a product is hampered somewhat by Web browsers that are not yet sophisticated enough to handle this interactivity.

One of the commercial experiments with interactive television is to combine live sporting events with associated Internet activities, such as analysis of plays on the field, court, course or track. An argument could be made that the visual may well end up being the gateway to the word, once the convergence of technologies is complete.

The answer to the generation gap won't all be in the technology. The machines are simply tools for new distribution channels, and those channels are merely ways to reach the new news communities for young adults. They are tools to help bridge a generation gap. The question is: Who will build the bridge?

The global generation

Robert Klein, former executive producer for KRON-TV in San Francisco, has tried to build that bridge for years, through a TV project with the working title, "The Global Teen-ager." Klein has tapped into the way that U.S. consumer markets for clothing, movies and music drive global demand.

Travel the world and discover that Klein's basic premise is clear. Japanese culture dictates that schoolchildren wear uniforms: white shirts and blue skirts or trousers. But within those parameters are many variations in a society said to value conformity: a buzz cut; gelled hair; rolled-up shirt sleeves; pleated, baggy trousers. Clearly, U.S. influence is felt worldwide.

What is less clear, at least in the eyes of major U.S. corporations, is the way in which the world has influenced young Americans, too, witness Pokémon mania. For all the laments about the decline of foreign-news coverage, especially on television, a burgeoning ethnic-language press is growing, deeply engaged in international issues.

U.S. immigration is high. A growing portion of young people know different languages. They have relatives abroad. They travel to and from their native lands. The U.S. Census Bureau reported 25.8 million foreign-born U.S. adults in 1998, up from 14 million in 1980. At the turn of the last century, immigration was a boon to newspapers: Immigrants would read the papers to learn to be American. Today, editors view the same circumstance negatively: Immigrants don't want to read mainstream papers because of language and cultural barriers.

Other professions have managed to broaden their horizons. The medical profession relied heavily for years on immigrants, both doctors and nurses, especially from Asia. Internet industries rely heavily on computer engineers from India. You're more likely to hear National Public Radio in a Washington, D.C., taxi with a West African driver than in a congressional office. Beauty businesses pull heavily from old Soviet states, Ireland and Korea. Even advertising is on to this trend. A year or so ago, AT&T changed the mother's location in its "call your mom" long-distance commercials. She's more likely to be in Southern Asia than in the Deep South.

A growing number of students, young and mobile, help push the international youth interest. Internationalism is growing among U.S. students, too, especially those from good universities. Fifty years ago these young people might have gone to Paris to hang out, write and paint. A decade ago they went to Eastern Europe, Poland mostly, to exploit the fall of communism. A few years ago they chose Hong Kong and Singapore for investment banking. Even those now staying home to start dot-com companies find their businesses quickly swimming in international commerce. The Internet has made the global village real.

What all this means is that the world as portrayed in traditional media is more remote and less relevant than the world many young people know. The adage in politics is, "Think globally, act locally." In the news media, we seem to have the local part right. What about the global part? How do the traditional, locally focused media open new windows on the world for the young?

Take this job and ...

Any hope of narrowing the gender gap at traditional news organizations will require young journalists, not just for coverage but also for designing new formats and new approaches to storytelling. Unless the next wave of news investment is directed toward human resources rather than technical ones, this task will be difficult indeed. In a full-employment economy, entry-level reporting is among the worst-paying jobs college graduates can take.

The most recent Radio-Television News Directors Association/Ball State University survey found entry-level annual salaries in radio and television news averaging less than $20,000. Print reporters and editors started at about $24,000. Paralegals averaged nearly $30,000, computer engineers $40,000.

Fewer students appear to be training for news jobs, especially for television news. The Annual Survey of Journalism and Mass Communications Enrollments found the number of students in college broadcast programs declining for the third straight year, from 12.4% of enrollment in 1995 to 9.9% in 1996 and to 8.5% in 1997. The trend has continued. In 1999, smaller-market media companies reported difficulty filling jobs.

That leaves entry-level jobs to those who understand the opportunity best. But those who see journalism as a calling aren't always those who would do it best.

The best and the brightest have too many other opportunities in the information economy, including jobs at less formal companies that offer greater freedom. News organizations tend to be fairly traditional and hierarchical, making it more difficult for young people to make a difference.

Arthur Gelb, the retired *New York Times* managing editor who ran the city desk during the urban rebellions of the 1960s, reflected recently about the vigor and importance of young journalists in his (also my) newsroom back then. "It was wild," he said. "I didn't think I was an editor. I felt more like a lion tamer, unable to manage you all."

Even more than money, what many young dot-com entrepreneurs get today is capital to develop their ideas. Two companies stand out in this regard. Tribune Co. of Chicago made a $6 million early investment in AOL at the suggestion of a manager in Tribune Media Services. That stake has turned into more than $1.5 billion. The company also invested in BlackVoices.com, a reporter's brainchild. At Central Newspapers in Phoenix, the $30 million digital platform that has revolutionized its zoning and business operations began as an idea from a young assistant managing editor.

There are few places where journalists who are not executives can have that much influence on their institutions. Some don't want it, preferring to write stories and stay out of decision-making. But to compete for talent, news media must offer such opportunities. By doing so they can attract young people with the skill and vision to shape their companies for future audiences.

Noted gerontologist Robert N. Butler said recently that given the size and importance of some of the country's biggest companies, he forgets there is a lifecycle for industries as well as humans.

"In a speech, I mentioned the endurance of American corporations, and a member of the audience politely corrected me," Butler recalled. "He said almost half of the companies in the Fortune 500 ceased to exist in 25 years. I checked. He was right. Some industries can survive change in maturity, but many others wither and die."

CHAPTER 5

Localism: Why the Internet and Bill Gates Can't Kill the Local Media Market

We like what is familiar and close. In the news business, that means local.

This remains true despite the dawn of the global village, growing national advertising and the hundreds of billions of dollars generated by dot-com companies.

With a few exceptions (some quite large), fundamental social and economic forces support the local-market focus for newspapers, radio and television — and the Internet will follow suit. Niche markets will proliferate but won't replicate local media's market power.

As online access approaches 50% penetration at home and work, local Web sites make more economic sense to news providers. Profits may be years away, but local news solidifies customer relationships. The Internet hasn't changed that.

"The Internet growth rate at the local level is much higher than at the national level," said James Calloway, acting president and publisher of Nando Media, an online information and service provider in Raleigh, N.C. From September 1998 to September 1999, the number of visitors has been about flat to The Nando Times, the McClatchy Co.'s well-regarded national and international Web site serving nine of its 11 daily newspapers. In contrast, visitors to U.S. daily newspapers' locally oriented Web sites increased between 15% and 100% during the same period, according to *Editor & Publisher*.

Community newspapers report similar explosive growth. They're booming by providing Web sites to clubs, sports teams, families and civic organizations — all linked to the newspaper's portal site. This self-organizing audience will eventually produce dollars from advertising or e-commerce.

How will this local growth change the Internet picture? Will a series of local communities build into a whole nation like the small bits of color in an impressionist painting? In time. But that isn't the way things are now.

National and local market cycles

Electronic media often start with small local experiments, then quickly go national because they require specific delivery devices and economies of scale. When people first adopt new technology, too few are using the devices (radios, televisions, computers) to make local markets profitable. Initial costs for programming and selling advertising are too great to support local efforts. This was true in the early days of the printing press, the first hand presses being reserved for national purposes, but it's especially and increasingly true in the electronic age.

As new technologies or regulations changed market economics, local markets eventually made more sense. Three television networks became five or six, plus cable. Channel choices grew from three to more than 50 in most markets. Local programming, including news, became more important.

Print media experienced the same dynamic, and today's market is in its most mature, most local stages. The national audience and ad base for print media seems finite. Those who entered and developed it first have become dominant — the first-to-market advantage. *The Wall Street Journal* and newsmagazines had decades of advantage in the national news market before *The New York Times* and *USA TODAY* developed the technology, sales channels and brand to compete successfully.

On the Internet, Yahoo!, America Online and amazon.com are among the first-to-market entrants working hard to solidify national front-runner status in providing news, information and entertainment, and in offering e-commerce.

Even when the focus is national, a bit of the impressionist style shows through. AOL's Digital Cities sites, in conjunction with local news media, provide local directories. And one-third of Nando's advertising consists of national ads for local sites, Calloway said.

A national business's long-term viability depends on the nature of its products. Selling services is different from selling goods. Delivering lightweight compact discs, books, drugs or even computers is very different from trucking around major appliances. Early e-commerce successes were in light or even weightless products and transactions. Now, many Internet retailers are busy building distribution warehouses, which could raise operating costs significantly or affect consolidated distribution systems. Automobiles, for example, have been national brands sold through local dealerships, but Internet activity is changing these relationships. By 2003, nearly 8 million new-car purchases will be influenced by the Net; of these, half a million will be transacted entirely online. As a result, some manufacturers are buying up independent dealerships — a controversial practice at odds with franchise regulations. Those who believe the future will be in a national or international media market point to these developments.

....

PERCENTAGE OF STATIONS AND NEWSPAPERS WITH WEB SITES

TV Stations	82%
Radio Stations	62%
Newspapers	64%

Source: RTNDA/Ball State University, NAA

....

Geography does affect a media business's nature, size and growth. In broadcasting, regional tastes drive station success. In publishing, numerous executives have wasted untold millions challenging natural, cultural or political geography.

Desktop publishing and the Internet promise to upset this order by cutting publishing costs and by creating nongeographic communities of interest. To some extent, they already have. Interest-group newsletters, international bridge clubs, online chat rooms and the like have grown and competed with traditional media for the public's attention to information and entertainment. Information — news and ideas — float freely around the world, but the economic systems supporting the flow still are rooted in advertising, in goods and services purchased by efficient local markets.

Advertising, especially that of newspapers, is organized around local commerce. Retailers traditionally advertise in media whose audience lives within five miles of their stores. Online shopping is expected to make up only about 6% of retail by 2003, a huge number of dollars but a small fraction of commerce. Shopping remains a social activity for many people, hence the American mall. Burgeoning online shopping for the 1999 holiday season did not stymie sales growth for traditional bricks-and-mortar stores.

Daily newspaper editions reflect the local commercial pattern. Food sections on Wednesday or Thursday correspond to the day fresh food reached a market, historically. Friday entertainment ads allow readers to plan weekend leisure. Real estate and automobile sections run on weekends, when people have time to contemplate major purchases. Employment listings run on Sunday, when job seekers plan their application week.

Because lifestyle patterns drive media patterns, most commerce is local. Distribution patterns make it one thing to find an out-of-print book or rare movie poster on the Internet but quite another to get a good deal there on a used freezer — and get it delivered.

Television, then the Internet, go local

The local-national-local life cycle applies especially to television. First, experimental stations cropped up. Next, the networks ruled. Today's leader, by any indicator, is the local station.

Local TV news is the most watched and most credible news medium, outranking networks or local and national newspapers with the public. Prime-time audiences rise and fall on the strength of local evening newscasts. The station with the best local news usually delivers that market's best network audience.

More importantly, TV stations find a growing proportion of their revenue coming from local advertising. While slightly more than half of TV

....

Broadcast Television

MYTHS:
• People watch cable news, not network news.
• Local and network TV news offers little beyond crime and tabloid-style sensationalism.

REALITY:
• Fewer people watch network news, but viewership still exceeds 25 million households — 10 times the usual audience for the all-news cable channels.
• Some network news programs are growing, notably the morning news shows, for which networks have invested heavily in new studios and talent.
• The public rates local TV news as the most credible news medium.

ISSUES:
• What is the best financial model for network television in this era of media convergence, audience fracture and industry consolidation?
• How big an audience can network broadcasters hope to hold?
• How will advertisers value these viewers, especially for news programs, which tend to attract audiences older than the most-coveted advertising targets?
• What will be the financial relationships between networks and their affiliates concerning programming costs? Historically, networks pay stations

"compensation" to carry programming, but a San Francisco-area station has agreed instead to pay NBC for the programs it carries.
• What is the future of the nightly network newscast, especially at ABC and CBS, neither of which owns a sister cable-news channel to share production costs?
• What will happen to news at local stations now that the FCC allows a single company to own two TV stations in the same city? Already in Jacksonville, Fla., ownership consolidations may result in a single newscast for two stations.
• How would a wholesale repeal of the cross-ownership rule — to allow newspapers to own same-market TV stations or vice versa and share news resources — affect local coverage?

TRENDS:
• Local stations have become more powerful than networks, and nowhere is that truer than in news programming. The local station with the best local news usually gets the highest overall ratings, and its profit margins are often double those of newspapers.
• As local stations expand news offerings, they gain advertisers and credibility. The Fox network has made local news broadcasts a condition of affiliation.
• At the network level, NBC has devel-

revenue has come from local dollars in the past, 1999 estimates push that percentage to between two-thirds and three-fourths. As a result, stations are expanding their local news — generally the only local programming produced. Already, local news programming runs as long as four hours a day in some markets. Stations have early-morning, mid-morning, noon, mid-afternoon, evening and late-night newscasts. Moreover, about 40% of the nation's TV stations planned newscast expansions in 1998, according to an

oped the most successful and complete news operation with its combination of network, local-affiliate and cable-news channels. Only Fox is positioned to replicate it.

• Broadcasters have been more successful than big-brand print publishers as Internet Web-site operators.

• Spanish-language television (and radio) are gaining dominance. Univision's network news is a market leader in Miami and, sometimes, Los Angeles.

• High-definition television service, mandated by federal regulation, is taking longer to develop than predicted.

WATCH FOR THIS:

• Broadcasters will keep merging and consolidating to capitalize on new ownership rules.

• More affiliates will pay networks to carry programming.

• As broadband access grows, network partnerships with Internet portals will too.

• Media convergence (the drive to distribute multiple forms of media through a single device or "box") could change the very nature of broadcasting, especially as it relates to news.

• NBC must decide whether to continue to build its news operation — the largest among the networks in terms of TV broadcast and cable programming — or whether to build its entertainment business. It is the only broadcast or cable news network without its own film studio.

• ABC and CBS (Viacom) must decide whether to expand news operations as their networks become smaller pieces of larger entities.

• Broadcasters face important choices concerning digital-spectrum use between now and the time high-definition television takes hold in U.S. households — such as whether to offer separate newscasts simultaneously.

• The public will adopt new technologies that could change substantially the interaction between viewers and programs. Among them: interactive television and digital VCRs that are extremely easy to use.

"BIG THREE" NETWORKS' PRIME-TIME AUDIENCE SHARE

1950	1960	1970	1980	1990	1997
0.84	0.92	0.91	0.88	0.63	0.54

Source: TV Dimensions

RTNDA/Ball State University survey. Locally and regionally, all-news cable channels are gaining audience and ad revenue as well.

The local-television financial picture is far rosier than that of the broadcast networks and their proliferating competitors. In fact, local stations have been so profitable — with margins averaging 45% for owned and operated affiliates — that networks toyed with getting out of the programming business altogether. With costs skyrocketing, and before recent regulatory changes that allowed networks to again own a financial stake in their programming, NBC has been the only consistently profitable network among the "big three."

The networks didn't want to abandon television completely; they just wanted to unload their programming services and keep their local "owned and operated" stations for their high financial returns. Newscasts account for the largest single piece of affiliate-station profits, averaging about 40% of the total. The cost of adding a half-hour or so of news to the schedule is usually cheaper than filling the time with syndicated programming, and the additional coverage bolsters the stations' Web sites.

The Internet, too, is in the throes of a national-to-local cycle, with a few twists.

As homes first signed on to the Internet over the past two years, national service made sense. Now the logic is changing, said Calloway of Nando Media.

"When we started, Internet access was at about 10% penetration. If our newspapers had, say, 200,000 subscribers — pretty deep into our markets — we'd be talking, at most, 40,000 Web users in that city," he said. "That's respectable but not enough on its own. But the 40,000 potential users across a number of markets aggregated to an audience we could sell to advertisers." Enter the national phase. Today, with the growing prevalence of the Internet in homes and offices, he said, the dynamic is moving to local marketing, even though no one yet fully understands the best local niches to fill online.

Meanwhile, local news has become critical to the big Internet sites. MSNBC's information-based Web site has the largest audience among traditional news brands and is betting on local news for its growth strategy, said Steven J. White, director of product planning and research. MSNBC is commissioning proprietary wire reports to fill the local-news void in key markets whose NBC affiliates lack Web sites. MSNBC's Web site is adding local streaming video newscasts, reinforcing its brand identity as a supplier of local news.

The new wrinkle: behemoth portals vie for local appeal
Internet portal sites on the Web are the new gatekeepers of online news, information and entertainment. Their power relies on a paradox of the digital information world: While cyberspace is infinite, entrance to it is linear and mediated. Everyone sees that all-important first screen.

Through technology and sheer brute market power, portals have been controlled by multibillion-dollar international companies — those that provide computer operating systems, Web browsers and the like. This phenomenon blurs the progression of mass media from local experiments to national and back to local. The question: Will a new local/national hybrid emerge?

One budding example is *The Washington Post,* which deeply penetrates its local market. It announced its intention to become a portal and to create an exclusive cable partnership with MSNBC. This helps the *Post* solidify both its local power and its national reputation for political coverage during the 2000 election campaign.

As the Internet has grown into its mass-market, national stage, AOL, Yahoo!, Excite and Lycos have become brand-name giants by attracting millions of unique visitors each month. As a result, some 90% of advertising dollars that followed human eyeballs onto the World Wide Web went to behemoth sites such as these. They seem to be in the driver's seat, leading the race to provide the most powerful first screens.

Yet local media Web sites have these advantages over the national portals:

• Newspaper, television and radio operators can promote their own sites — exposure that portals pay hundred of millions of dollars to replicate. Eighty-two percent of the nation's TV stations, 62% of radio stations and 64% of daily newspapers have Web sites.

• After fits and starts, a more sophisticated sales and marketing apparatus for online advertising is growing and supporting alternatives to national portals in the Internet marketplace.

• The faster the world moves, the more familiarity resonates among people, and that means local media.

KOZ.com in Durham, N.C., intends to capitalize on the familiarity factor via its flagship product, the Community Publishing System. CPS gives local media and community groups the tools, templates and services to create interactive online newspapers, message boards, chat rooms and other features.

Most Internet communities "attempt to create something from nothing," said KOZ.com's co-founder, Frank A. Daniels III. "Internet users will not spontaneously form a cohesive, organic unit simply because their Web pages have been grouped together on a file server. The true challenge for achieving online community is to overcome the fragmentation of the Internet membership base by building online communities that are extensions of actual geographic, local communities."

As Internet penetration grows, a national mass-marketing system makes sense and will for some time, despite growing dissatisfaction with that system. The advertising clutter frustrates portal users, who are frequently online for a specific purpose. Advertisers are not getting as much traffic to their sites as they expected in the early, everything-is-amazing dawn of the Internet. So,

Webmeisters suddenly must contend with two grumbling customer groups.

For its part, the advertising industry has not built an effective sales system for the new medium. If a customer wants an online audience, the simple answer has been to buy a huge portal audience and hope for the best. "It's the natural human tendency of the media buyer to make one buy for one million impressions, rather than 10 buys of 100,000," said Nando Media's Calloway.

But that is changing. Because the Internet is an interactive medium, advertisers can measure results from the "click-through" responses for sales, even if they cannot target potential customers as directly as they hoped.

Consumer responses from national sites are declining, however, due to too much clutter and too many choices. So, while advertising flowed to a few major portals in the past, it is slowly moving to more discretely identified sites.

Historically, that's what local media companies are good at: discerning and selling discrete audience segments to advertisers. Internet marketing firms

....

Cable Television

MYTH:
• The main thing cable TV does is provide clear broadcast signals, along with some special programming.

REALITY:
• Cable is, in fact, the most powerful communications medium today — one with great reach and control of content. If current trends hold, it promises to become more so.
• Cable continues to grow in advertising revenue and audience.

ISSUES:
• Cable is in a race with telephone companies to wire U.S. homes with high-speed connections called broadband. Antitrust suits have charged cable companies with unfair monopoly control over consumer access to Internet services.
• Unlike phone companies, cable operators can control content, including the number of news channels on their systems and, possibly, the portals and navigational pathways consumers use online.
• Given the cable mergers with phone companies, will government regulators force cable to function again as a common carrier, giving up or reducing control over programming?

TRENDS:
• More homes now subscribe to cable services than to daily newspapers, and cable fees make up the biggest portion of per capita media expenditures.
• MSNBC often attracts the largest cable-news audiences on breaking events, and the Fox News Channel sometimes leads in prime time, beating pioneer CNN, which is available in more homes.
• Internet users watch more cable and less broadcast news than viewers not connected to the Web.
• Local all-news cable stations are gaining in number, popularity and advertising revenue.
• With each demand for new chan-

have sprung up to help Web sponsors analyze online behavior patterns. Because some online pricing is based on "click-throughs," the actual response to banners, the differential value of national portals and local ones should shake out over time.

Understanding the potential, content providers and advertisers are increasingly emphasizing local media portals. Excite@Home, an Internet broadband portal, dedicates one-quarter of its first screen — its portal — to a local content partner. Knight Ridder's Real Cities online information service began as a national brand but found that the only way to become truly national was to build a network of local and regional sites.

Change is still percolating. Traditional news sites rank far down on the national list of sites attracting the most Web visitors. Broadcast brands come first, then national newspaper brands, and local news-media brands follow.

---

nels, cable operators cut the number of homes receiving C-SPAN, the nonprofit public-affairs system that covers Congress live.

WATCH FOR THIS:

• Government will initiate more antitrust lawsuits and rule-making as cable operators sign up more homes for broadband access and portal navigation.

• Newspapers, local broadcast stations and cable companies will combine resources to form larger regional cable news networks and Web sites for all-news, cross-media operations. A.H. Belo Corp.'s Texas Cable Network and Tribune Co.'s ChicagoLand Television are early examples.

• CNN, the most mature cable news provider, will face a difficult challenge in competing against the new crop of rival news challengers.

• Cable will feature more broadcast reruns of all types as network owners make new deals with affiliate stations defining what can be retransmitted, outside of old-fashioned syndication agreements.

• Cable news channels will try to grow audience share for their regularly scheduled programming.

ESTIMATED CABLE REVENUE AND CASH FLOW PER SUBSCRIBER

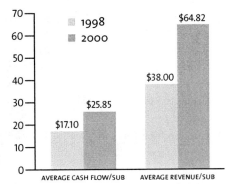

Source: "Digital Decade," Morgan Stanley Witter

A tale of two city ventures

Two years ago virtually every big-city publisher scurried to protect itself from Sidewalk, Microsoft's Internet city guide. They feared that Microsoft would pull business away from daily newspapers by developing news and an advertising base via this entertainment-based channel. Last summer, however, Microsoft abandoned the effort and sold Sidewalk to USA Network's Ticketmaster.

Former Sidewalk Publisher Frank Schott said Microsoft planned to use its superior technology and market reach to build local Web sites around local entertainment offerings. Users would sign on at work to plan their leisure activities based on information including Sidewalk's movie reviews and up to 800 local restaurant ratings. An independent sales force would market advertising to small merchants based on a directory model, like the Yellow Pages. Tracking software would help Sidewalk build business. It seemed like a great plan. But it didn't work for Microsoft.

"We got seduced into a medium that afforded unlimited amounts of data at a time when people hadn't figured out how deep information needs to be," Schott said. "We thought we would win because we had the most comprehensive list of data ... but I wish we had built a site that was less content-rich and more nimble. We could have done it for at least one-third less." In other words, content overtook concept. Deep local content proved too expensive to produce on a national scale.

Sidewalk's full-service model stopped at 10 sites, and Microsoft offered pared-down sites in 70 cities as local content on its MSN portal. Eventually, rival Ticketmaster bought it.

Although Microsoft brought great resources to the local directory market, Sidewalk offered nothing really new. Its technology did not improve sales efficiency. It did not offer better search capability to allow small advertisers to attract more customers. It did not build a discrete brand. It did not capture the imagination of the public or serve its needs with a unique product.

KRON-TV in San Francisco did. Long before the advent of local cable news, KRON created an early partnership with CNN to provide a 5-minute, zoned, local report at the end of each half-hour of CNN Headline News. KRON General Manager Amy McCombs saw the opportunity to meld local to national and went for it. KRON's move was one of several the station made to bolster its voice in one of the nation's most fractured and competitive media markets.

KRON built partnerships with various local media, including the *San Francisco Chronicle,* which was owned in common until recently. In 1995, KRON put the pieces together with a series, "About Race," which aired on the 6 p.m. local news and was discussed every morning on KRON's cable channel. The *Chronicle* published polls, editorials and op-ed pieces on the subject. Public radio station KQED-FM broadcast ongoing conversations on the series and the subject. The marketwide series became a model for regional issue coverage, which later tackled mayoral elections and public transportation.

KRON's value as a deeply local institution and NBC affiliate created record bids when the station went on the auction block in the sale of its owner, Chronicle Publishing. It sold for almost $850 million in November 1999 to Young Broadcasting Co., a record.

Gannett: a local, contrarian strategy

The Gannett Co. has turned the local-national-local media life cycle into billions of dollars in business. *USA TODAY* is national and sexy, but Gannett never lost sight of the fundamental importance of local dominance.

Gannett owns more than 70 daily newspapers with a combined daily paid circulation of more than 6 million, including *USA TODAY* — some 10% of all U.S. daily circulation. Gannett papers and broadcast properties are extremely local in focus. Digitally, the company is buying time, riding the national wave with *USA TODAY's* site while quietly mining local marketplaces and avoiding too large a step, or the wrong step, or the right step too soon.

Gannett has pared its newspaper portfolio and swapped papers to create regional clusters, such as one covering southern New Jersey. Along those lines, Gannett has developed three parallel marketing functions, separate from advertising or circulation but supporting both, according to Michelle J. Foster, Gannett's vice president for newspaper market development:

• Market data to assess market segments and sales targets, with "opportunity analysis" to measure prospects for business growth.

• The Targeting Knowledge program, which develops customer relationships by managing the "Five P's" — product, promotion, placement, pricing and personnel.

• Sales programs that support reader prospecting and retention.

Within this framework, Gannett's technological rush is not to capture eyeballs it already has but to quietly prepare its business practices for new opportunities. Years ago, it moved away from traditional circulation managers and hired executives with marketing backgrounds instead. Its proprietary computerized market-modeling system, Genesys, provides many more options for building advertising and circulation than most local newspapers have.

This system moves Gannett papers away from the usual sales benchmarks, including one suggesting that a newspaper's revenue should equal about 1% of a market's retail sales. Genesys precisely measures local business segments: How big are they? How much do they usually spend on advertising? How much can the newspaper expect to garner? The program shifts the sales-development focus from national averages to community specifics. Gannett

> **As the online market fills in, and telecommunications companies consolidate their holdings, they will need local partners. Local news drives traffic; classified ads drive commerce. Even a national sales channel is only as good as its local links.**

also uses the model to analyze potential acquisitions based on a town's commercial opportunities.

But the definition of local is not static. In New York's Westchester, Putnam and Rockland counties, for example, Gannett melded nine newspapers and 12 editions into one title with five editions, *The Journal News,* in October 1998. The change brought mixed results. Annual circulation declined 4.5% daily and 2.1% on Sunday, Editor Robert W. Ritter said. But the broader coverage within a local area is attracting younger readers who had never subscribed, primarily those 35 to 40 years old, especially those devoted to New York City publications. Circulation has been on the rebound since June 1999, Ritter said.

"We needed countywide newspapers to serve our readers and be able to consolidate government knowledge," he said. "If the Peekskill school board was working on a problem shared by Yonkers, the people in Yonkers would never see the coverage. We felt that was a mistake."

Gannett also slowed development of content-rich Internet sites in small markets, choosing instead to put Internet operations under marketing-department control to protect classified advertising until the company figures out what Internet information sites are all about.

"We look at the Internet more from a traditional view, rather than a futuristic one. It's a resource question," said Gannett's vice president of business development, John A. Williams.

The strategy is controversial within the company, especially among editors, who believe that richer content sites would help circulation marketing by building the local brand. Gannett's urban papers, such as *The Des Moines* (Iowa) *Register,* do have robust Web sites, linked to the *USA TODAY* site. *FLORIDA TODAY* in Melbourne is closely tied to the space program and carries launches live via online video. But the company sees no coherent strategy yet for the Web sites in its smaller markets, which have some local news and a great deal of local commerce.

For Williams, the issue is not just cost but how to provide journalism in this environment. "If we could post online school board meeting results a half hour after the meeting, then we have quality, we have value-added," he said.

But in small markets, as in New York's northern suburbs, newspapers might find no competitive advantage to being early with a local Internet news strategy, all things being equal.

Local consolidation may be key to success

Recreating the mass market in today's fractured media environment has come most easily to the few national Web sites and portals. They were new brands to early subscribers.

But as the online market fills in and telecommunications companies consolidate their holdings, they will need local partners. Local news drives traffic; classified ads drive commerce. Even a national sales channel is only as good as its local links. Classified Ventures, the online service that links the classified advertising of participating newspapers, has found that out. Even with its local newspaper partners, it needed more aggressive local sales to grow in new product categories that some newspapers had not sold before. Apartment rentals is one such category.

So while local newspapers and broadcast stations are natural local affiliates to the big national converged media, they won't necessarily prevail without becoming even more local.

Regulatory impediments have made it difficult for media to consolidate locally. Newspapers and broadcast stations cannot be owned in common, and fully competing newspapers cannot purchase each other in patterns that reduce competition. Tribune Co.'s pending $8 billion acquisition of Times Mirror challenges those rules directly, creating newspaper-television combinations in New York, Los Angeles and Hartford, Conn., in addition to its long-held cross-media operations in Chicago. (See chapter 7 for a discussion of the rules.)

Historically, large newspapers find it too inefficient to report community news or to sell advertising to small businesses. That's why community weeklies have thrived.

In the electronic world, advertisers might compete directly against the media they traditionally used for marketing and sales. As the Internet becomes a more efficient way to sell classified ads, for example, one of newspapers' biggest customer groups, Realtors, are creating an exclusive Web site for listings that previously ran in newspapers.

All this suggests that even locally embedded media must change in the big new digital world. The question is: Which entities have the wherewithal to do it?

One way for newspaper companies to create local efficiency is to dominate not just a city but a region. Knight Ridder, for example, publishes a daily in one county adjoining its flagship *San Jose* (Calif.) *Mercury News* and publishes weeklies in another. The Washington Post Co. owns a string of suburban newspapers ringing Washington. MediaNews Group has surrounded the *Los Angeles Times* with local dailies and cooperatively delivers ad supplements with the *Times*. With grandfathered cross-ownership between print and broadcast companies joined by local cable and Web operations, the *Chicago Tribune* and *The Dallas Morning News* have multimedia local operations.

TV stations are beginning to consolidate, too, now that the FCC allows companies to own two stations within the same market (called duopoly) under certain circumstances.

As regulation recedes, the possibility exists for local media companies to consolidate functions more fully, thereby providing bigger numbers and deeper penetration into metropolitan markets. These companies have the most at stake and arguably the most daunting challenges to face — which could also render the job too difficult to pull off.

CHAPTER 6

Federal Policy: The Wild Card

It began simply: "Congress shall make no law ... abridging freedom of speech, or of the press." The nation has mostly kept faith with the First Amendment's spirit, protecting an unfettered flow of individual expression and information. The business of news, on the other hand, is continually subject to federal laws and rules that determine much about what we read and hear.

Journalists pride themselves on a few big press-freedom successes. These began most famously with challenges to the Alien and Sedition acts of 1798, under which 10 editors were convicted for coverage preceding the nation's war with France. Thomas Jefferson's election brought repeal of those laws. Recently, the most notable confrontation centered on the Nixon administration's attempts to prevent publication of the Pentagon Papers in 1971. Nixon failed. Freedom reigned. These are the celebrated First Amendment battles.

Far more important, and more insidious, are a host of laws, rules and policies affecting the way media companies do business.

More often than not, this federal engineering creates a marketplace of winners and losers. Broadcast and cable operators are thoroughly regulated, living and dying by these policies. But a number of laws also affect newspapers, which are assumed to be "unregulated" but must adhere to general rules governing commerce.

At times, newspapers gained mightily. The first Postmaster General, Benjamin Franklin, a prolific publisher himself, instituted the postal regulations that financially favored newspaper delivery through the mail, including distribution of his own publications. During the nation's western expansion, territories had to publish at least two dailies to qualify for statehood. Even in their market maturity, newspapers benefited for awhile from the 1970 Newspaper Preservation Act, which allowed dailies in the same market to form joint-operating arrangements for business purposes, while keeping newsrooms separate and competitive.

Other policies have been less helpful. The estate-tax structure encouraged the sales of smaller, family-owned media properties to conglomerates. Taxes got so high that families sold instead of trying to bequeath a heavily taxed business to the next generation. Those laws have eased over the years, but the pattern was set. Conglomerates themselves grew, in part, because of tax laws that made debt more profitable than equity investment. Remember the era of junk bonds and leveraged buyouts? The 1986 tax-code changes reversed those trends and caused many corporations to go bankrupt. They affected few media companies but many of their advertisers.

The government cites several reasons for its tinkering: to encourage a diversity of community voices; to curb monopoly power or market dominance; to husband a limited electromagnetic spectrum; and generally to support the "public interest." Here's how the regulatory nannies in Congress, the FCC and the Justice Department have lately made their impact felt:

• They deregulated cable TV earlier and more completely than broadcast television, and broadcasters are still trying to catch up.

• They continue to apply traditional antitrust standards to newspapers seeking to consolidate fractured markets while developing more liberal rules for broadcasters.

• To encourage local telephone competition and broadband Internet build-out, they allow megamergers among telecommunications companies — mergers that critics claim will limit competition and harm consumers.

• To encourage high-definition television (HDTV), they granted additional free-channel spectrum to broadcasters, giving them two channels, until 2006, at least.

Far-ranging effects

By definition, overarching policy debates substantially change the media marketplace. But so do smaller, less publicized actions.

One recent example: the price of prime-time television programming. As entertainment programs became more expensive to produce, TV news-magazines proliferated on broadcast networks. Lower production costs make nonfiction more immediately profitable. In the midst of this, however, the FCC reversed itself and allowed networks to hold financial interests in the programming they run. The new policy changed the formula.

Generally, a TV series makes serious money only with syndication. This usually requires four seasons of network episodes to create enough inventory to sell in off-hours or to cable networks. Broadcast networks, with a stake in ratings but not in the programs themselves, quickly cast off any series that failed to be an early hit. An instantly popular series also became instantly expensive. In a world in which print media commanded revenue from sub-

> **The government cites several reasons for its tinkering: to encourage a diversity of community voices; to curb monopoly power or market dominance; to husband a limited electromagnetic spectrum; and generally to support the public interest.**

scriptions and advertising, and cable operators got that and invested directly in the programs they carried, broadcasters were left with one income source, advertising, built around a shrinking audience.

Television newsmagazines became a less expensive alternative. For NBC, they solved an even bigger programming problem by providing cost-free content for its cable channels. The new rules allowing a financial stake in program production are taking the pressure off of news divisions. More new comedic and dramatic series are being developed as well as game shows. The latest front in the broadcast-news wars moved to the morning — which is, as newspapers have learned, a good time to sell nonfiction. The law of unintended consequences strikes the news again.

More examples? Here are a few among dozens:

• In 1997, the Federal Drug Administration for the first time approved the advertising of prescription drugs on television. More than $1 billion in pharmaceutical advertising flowed into traditional mass media, representing a 165% increase in medical-category spending, which continues to grow by about 40% a year. It's been Viagra for television — at the expense of newspapers, it turns out.

• The FCC loosened TV-station ownership rules. A single company could have five television and radio stations, then 12, and more recently any number whose audience does not exceed 35% of the U.S. population.

• In August 1999, the FCC relaxed rules limiting what the agency calls "duopolies" — two TV stations in the same market under a single company's ownership. Previous rules limited companies to one TV station per market. It deregulated radio-station ownership years ago, and profitable industry consolidation followed.

• The FCC approved mergers, including long-distance carrier AT&T's acquisition of cable operator Telecommunications Inc., joining long-distance capabilities with high-speed cable Internet access.

• Congress passed the direct-broadcast service bill, which for the first time allowed satellite services to carry local broadcast signals into the home, a new and frontal challenge to cable dominance.

Coming up, the FCC and other agencies will decide the fate of a proposed merger between AT&T and Media One, another giant cable operator. Also on regulators' plate is the proposed merger between MCI Worldcom and Sprint, historic rivals in the long-distance phone wars; between media giants Viacom and CBS; and between AOL and Time Warner.

Each decision could rearrange the communications landscape. But how will they affect the future of news? How important are they to news audiences? Will there be more and better news or less and inferior brands? The tangled legal and regulatory underbrush becomes clearer when viewed from a higher, more issue-based vantage point.

Wanted: customer access

The distribution conduit might prove as important as the content. AT&T, for example, allows broadband cable access to the Internet only through the Excite@Home portal. Since AT&T is now the largest cable supplier, the arrangement hurts other content-based portals. Numerous other Internet providers, including America Online, complained. AOL's merger with Time Warner would possibly alleviate the problem: Time Warner is the No. 2 operator of cable systems. Possibly in a pre-emptive move, Excite@Home's board of directors has itself chosen to separate content from connections, declaring its intention to allow other portals access in the future, once its exclusive arrangements have expired in 2002.

Pending government action will further define the electronic pathway into the home. The FCC has ruled that telephone companies must make their lines available to broadband entrepreneurs who provide DSL, or digital subscriber lines. If regular phone companies or DSL providers wire the home for high-speed service, cable modem access becomes less important.

The Microsoft antitrust case also has implications for the way online audiences evolve. In his April 2000 ruling, U.S. District Judge Thomas Penfield Jackson found that Microsoft violated antitrust laws, not only in the field of computer operating technology but also in using that dominance to control consumer access to the digital information world. One means is through automatic bundling of its Internet Explorer Web browser with the Windows operating systems — which, in turn, makes the Microsoft Network portal the first screen that many, if not most, Internet users see.

Jackson soon will issue the rest of his ruling on how Microsoft must remedy the situation. Microsoft has vowed to appeal.

No matter how the case ends, federal intervention has put brakes on the giant company, which also faces private class-action suits. Since Jackson's initial finding, for example, Microsoft gave up its battle to compete with AOL, now the largest online-news provider, for Internet instant-messaging service. AOL contended that Microsoft had "hacked its way" into AOL's proprietary messaging service, one of its strongest product attributes.

Though different, the AT&T, DSL and Microsoft issues all center on control over the first screen that appears when a consumer turns on an electronic device. News organizations have fought mightily to provide that first screen — or portal — or to be prominently represented there. The major online portals amass customers and the market power that comes with them. When settlement talks began early in 1999, Microsoft agreed to configure its Windows operating systems to allow other entities to program the first screen. Then it backed away. A stricter regulatory environment may yet accomplish that goal — in the courts, if not in Congress or the federal agencies.

The media-ownership "land rush"
On a national level, media companies are racing to consolidate. This isn't happening as quickly in local markets, where the debate over media concentration has taken center stage.

One reason for the local diversity is public policy that encourages numerous media "voices" in a community, especially in news. This goal has limited the ability of local competitors to buy each other, regardless of medium. When audience fragmentation nearly destroyed radio, the FCC reconsidered the rules and allowed multiple ownership of radio stations in a single market. Since then, radio consolidated and regained profitability. Companies can offer multiple niche formats in a single market while economizing with shared business operations.

In fall 1999, the FCC similarly relaxed the duopoly rules for TV stations. Now a single company can own two stations in a market, as long as at least eight other broadcast "voices" serve that market and both co-owned stations are not in the market's top four. Nor can a single owner's properties have more than 35% in collective national penetration. (Under this formula, UHF stations' audience share counts as only half that of VHF stations.) The policy change will spur ownership consolidation, especially in the largest markets. Under the new rules, Gannett, owner of the Jacksonville, Fla., NBC affiliate, announced it will buy the ABC affiliate there — then announced it will merge the stations' newsrooms. Under the plan, the ABC station would air simulcasts of the local NBC newscasts, except for one separate local newscast per day.

The FCC has yet to rescind its ban on newspaper and broadcast cross-ownership in the same market. The ban excludes only 21 cities where joint news-

For years, newspapers have called for a relaxation of cross-ownership rules. Now they're pushing hard. Media consolidation is the order of the day.

paper-broadcast ownership was grandfathered before the regulatory sanction took effect in 1975. These include Chicago, San Francisco, Atlanta and Dallas. The Washington Post Co. was in the original group, but it swapped stations with the company that owned *The Detroit News* before the FCC ruling, fearing it could be forced to sell under circumstances depressing the station's sale price.

The cross-ownership rules have shaped many media transactions. In 1983, for example, the Maynard family acquired *The Oakland Tribune* from the Gannett Co. because Gannett wanted to buy KRON-TV in San Francisco. Gannett never did buy the station, which the family-owned Chronicle Publishing Co. finally sold in November 1999 for $843 million to Young Broadcasting Inc., an independent company. Chronicle also sold its other largest property, the 134-year-old *San Francisco Chronicle,* for $660 million to the Hearst Corp., owner of the *San Francisco Examiner.* The *Chronicle,* the 12th-largest U.S. daily with 475,324 in average circulation, has been the *Examiner's* partner since 1965 in a joint-operating arrangement (JOA), under which they maintained separate news operations but jointly operated production, advertising, circulation and other noneditorial activities, sharing revenue and expenses 50-50. Hearst has sold the *Examiner,* although the courts have stayed the transaction, pending review.

Chronicle Publishing decided to sell in 1999 based on a strong economy, high prices for media properties and the Bay Area's economic growth. It also determined that its diverse assets could command higher prices if sold separately — the sales benefiting about three dozen fourth- and fifth-generation descendants of *Chronicle* founder M.H. de Young, none of whom remained in active management. Other company assets included two other dailies, in Massachusetts and Illinois, television and cable stations, and two book-publishing divisions.

Might KRON and the *Chronicle* have been sold together had cross-ownership rules been relaxed? That was not the agenda, said Hearst's chief news executive, George B. Irish. "Financially, that would be a big proposition," he commented. Young Broadcasting, the successful buyer, was up for sale itself before it acquired KCAL in Los Angeles and KRON. The big deals raised questions about whether Young, an otherwise small broadcaster, was positioning itself to cash in on future cross-ownership rule changes.

More deals shaped by cross-ownership rules: In 1986, when Gannett bought *The Detroit News,* cross-ownership rules required it to sell any TV stations owned by the *News'* parent company located in cities where Gannett published newspapers. Knight Ridder, owner of the *Detroit Free Press,* and Gannett soon formed a JOA. Knight Ridder bought almost all the disregarded Gannett stations. In another case, the FCC waived the rule to allow Rupert Murdoch's News Corp. to own New York City's local Fox television affiliate and the faltering *New York Post.* Currently, Tribune Co.'s pending acquisition of Times Mirror's newspapers would place cross-ownership under review anew. The purchase would create newspaper-broadcast operations in New York, Los Angeles and Hartford, Conn. The sale is possible because FCC rules allow companies to own both newspapers and televisions stations for a year or until the license is up for renewal, whichever is longer. Tribune station licenses in the target cities are good until 2006 and 2007, by which time any number of changes could take place. Also, Tribune has a historically sanctioned cross-ownership combination in Chicago and has sought approval to own permanently a Miami television station in addition to the *Sun-Sentinel* in nearby Fort Lauderdale.

For years, newspapers have called for a relaxation of cross-ownership rules. Now they're pushing hard, spurred on by Tribune Co.'s challenge. Media consolidation is the order of the day. Few remaining rules encumber national mergers. At the local level, cable rules have been relaxed for years. The recent relaxation of duopoly rules is fueling radio and television consolidation. Meanwhile, newspapers are "locked out of the scramble for broadcast stations, putting newspapers at a permanent and dramatic disadvantage," said John F. Sturm, president and CEO of the Newspaper Association of America. A number of measures were before Congress in fall 1999 to repeal the ban, and the industry also petitioned the FCC to act, but neither body had resolved the issue by April 2000, and conventional wisdom says the Clinton administration opposes lifting the ban.

The FCC "conceded that there could be a 'land rush for broadcasters,' which could be over quickly," Sturm explained of the change in the duopoly rule. "When this frantic acquisition dance begins, newspapers will be left on the sidelines, shackled by an arcane and unconstitutional regulation.

Meanwhile, others will be allowed to acquire a second television station plus, in some cases, up to six radio stations while the FCC keeps local newspaper publishers shut out. For the government to lock out local newspaper publishers is unfair, uncompetitive, and, frankly, bizarre in a world marked by hundreds of over-the-air and cable channels, broadcasting nationwide from satellites, and the ubiquitous nature of the Internet."

Given the importance of strong local news organizations to affiliate with growing national information networks, the future of cross-ownership is a key question indeed. Some would argue that the future of cross-ownership is the future of news. Almost every measure of news quality targets print as the seminal local media for enterprise journalism, providing myriad stories and ideas to local broadcasters. One publisher actually sued a radio station for repeating the newspaper's news too precisely over the air. In a climate of deregulation, the question is this: Can newspapers finally own these relationships?

Cable operators and broadcast networks are also banned from national cross-ownership, and cable operators and broadcast stations from local cross-ownership, but there is no active move under way to lift these bans.

Competing local dailies almost extinct

The new world of media consolidation has increased attacks on newspaper JOAs. Under pressure to reduce local print competition, the better to compete within the electronic media market, publishers in the few remaining JOA cities are colliding with community groups and courts bent on preserving the editorial voices of economically weak dailies.

Competing newspapers have merged throughout the century, especially during the financial doldrums of the Great Depression. In markets that couldn't support so many dailies, publishers had few choices: One newspaper bought out the other; they merged under a joint masthead; or they combined only their business operations, maintaining separate editorial products under separate ownership. The latter choice, the JOA, usually paired a dominant paper with a weaker one. As American work schedules and lifestyles changed, the morning newspapers generally grew stronger and their afternoon partners, weaker.

The first JOA was formed in Albuquerque in 1933, the last in York, Pa., in 1990. The 1970 Newspaper Preservation Act formally exempted these arrangements from antitrust laws, ostensibly to preserve editorial diversity in markets that could no longer support two competing dailies. JOAs formed in 28 cities. Fourteen remain in place, under contracts variously set to expire between now and 2090. Publishers in two of them, in Honolulu and San Francisco, are seeking early dissolution but face high legal hurdles to do so.

JOAs proved to be not so much vehicles to preserve newspapers permanently as they were mechanisms for phased consolidation. As the economic burden of supporting the weaker newspaper proved too great, it folded when the JOA expired.

In November, the 9th U.S. Circuit Court of Appeals enjoined plans to close the afternoon *Honolulu Star-Bulletin.* Gannett Pacific Corp., publisher of the morning *Honolulu Advertiser,* agreed to pay *Star-Bulletin* owner Liberty Newspapers $26.5 million to close the JOA partner instead of parceling out scheduled payments to Liberty until the JOA's 2012 expiration date. The appellate ruling supported state officials and a citizen group who have sued to prevent the shutdown.

The same court may face similar issues in San Francisco, over the Hearst Corp.'s purchase of its JOA partner, the *San Francisco Chronicle.* A sales contract for some *Examiner* assets had been signed – one that included healthy subsidies for three years from Hearst to the new owner, Ted Fang, publisher of a thrice-weekly competitor, *The Independent.* But as of April 2000, a judicial order stayed the sale of both newspapers. It was an action Hearst worked hard to prevent.

The U.S. Justice Department must approve each JOA dissolution, and that's a riddle in the regulatory game. Had Hearst announced its intent to purchase the *Chronicle* and continue publishing the *Examiner* as well, the Justice Department, understanding market dynamics, would have balked and assumed that Hearst actually intended to close the paper, Hearst executive Irish said. "In the San Francisco market, newspapers command about one-third of all advertising dollars, and the San Francisco newspapers receive only one-third of that," he said. So the company found a new owner. Ultimately, the courts saw this arrangement as a ruse as well.

Hearst is involved in another JOA battle. In March, the afternoon *Seattle Times* switched to morning publication, competing directly with Hearst's *Post-Intelligencer.* The move represents the first instance of JOA partners engaged in direct competition, and it led to early speculation that Hearst plans to abandon publishing there. But recent investments at the *Post-Intelligencer* quieted such discussion.

Spectrum wars: HDTV vs. C-SPAN, broadcast vs. cellular

Anyone who doubts the regulatory effect on news need only consider high-definition television, a major regulatory concern before it has even entered the average home. No single HDTV digital format has emerged, although broadcasters have chosen several.

The issue for broadcasters now is the status of their digital signals running on cable systems. There's quite a backdrop here: It took long court battles and new regulation to get cable operators to carry, and pay broadcasters for, their analog signals. For HDTV, each broadcaster would need a second channel for its digital signal. Legislation setting out digital television's growth has made it clear that broadcasters should have a second cable channel for digital. But which broadcasters? Would all stations in a market have the right to two signals on cable?

One potential loser in the digital must-carry debate is C-SPAN, which carries all sessions of Congress live, in addition to a host of civic events and public-affairs programs.

C-SPAN has been a talisman to the cable industry — a voluntary program that offers a kind of redeeming public value, no matter what else cable carries. Most cable operators pay for C-SPAN, but not all carry the service — at least not both of its channels.

"Since 1993, our public-service efforts have been, and continue to be, a victim of the must-carry rule," said Brian P. Lamb, C-SPAN's founder and chief executive officer. The first round of negotiations to accommodate broadcast signals resulted in the service being dropped from 10 million homes, he said. A second round of spectrum-sharing with broadcasters could further limit C-SPAN's availability.

C-SPAN's brief to the FCC said, in part, "There is absolutely no doubt that if broadcasters continue to have the benefit of a government-imposed preference for access to cable systems' limited channel capacity, and if that preference is expanded, then C-SPAN and C-SPAN 2's unique form of programming will disappear from households across the country."

Yet another odd couple of public policy:

The future of those local-news live shots — the ones critics hate — is tied to a reallocation of digital spectrum to expand cellular-phone services. In these negotiations — in shorthand, about ENG (Electronic News Gathering) spectrum — the FCC wants broadcasters to accommodate the nation's growing communications needs by cutting back on the spectrum they now use. To do so while continuing live, on-scene broadcasts, however, requires equipment changes. Who will pay for those and how much? Mostly, the satellite companies needing the new capacity would pay, but the devil is in the details, and the details are not worked out.

Other small but noteworthy broadcast issues concern low-powered radio, which transmits almost neighborhood-range radio signals, and digital audio transmission, which would let each broadcaster use the same electromagnetic spectrum to reach niche audiences. These, too, will be resolved not by the marketplace but in Washington.

The FCC voted in January 2000 to establish low-power stations, a decision that is under challenge by broadcasters and in Congress.

First Amendment advocates are sanguine about the future of free speech on the Internet. Ironically, they are riding the wave of a fierce Internet industry lobby that tries to block almost any legislative or regulatory restriction, including those related to content.

Internet rules: Will the Internet rule?

Certainly, a big regulatory agenda revolves around the Internet, its freedom, marketplace rules and privacy.

In 1996, Congress passed the Communications Decency Act, which prohibited certain Internet activities believed to put children at risk of encountering inappropriate information or predatory Internet users. The bill passed, with no news-industry objection, although some free-speech advocates challenged it in the courts. It was struck down by the U.S. Supreme Court the next year as unconstitutional. Congress passed a new version, which also has been challenged on free-speech grounds in the federal courts.

Meantime, Congress acted to ensure vigorous Internet growth. It passed an "anti-squatter" law prohibiting entrepreneurs from registering Web-site names that are easily identified with existing companies — then reselling the Internet addresses to those same companies at hefty prices.

Congress also has banned sales taxes on Internet transactions, a move that state and local authorities fear could seriously erode their tax-revenue bases. Estimates of e-commerce growth are large but represent a fraction of overall sales. Still, given the growing choices between online shopping and traditional sales, and depending on delivery charges, the absence of e-commerce sales taxes would make the virtual marketplace decidedly cheaper.

Numerous other attempts to rein in Internet businesses are pending, some related to content, others to commerce. They include: filtering offensive content out of the flow of information to schools and libraries; banning online sales of guns and alcohol; banning cyber-gambling; requiring cable companies to open broadband lines to competitors, and protecting information in computer databases. Expect more challenges to come.

First Amendment advocates are sanguine about the future of free speech on the Internet. Ironically, they are riding the wave of a fierce Internet industry lobby that tries to block almost any legislative or regulatory restriction, including those related to content.

"We're optimistic," said Michael Godwin, senior legal editor of E-Commerce Law Weekly and one of the lawyers who successfully challenged the Communications Decency Act. "There is a presumption against regulation that comes from the Internet industry lobby, and as to specific attempts to regulate content, case law has previously spoken on these issues."

Godwin said that he wouldn't object to laws protecting individual privacy from commercial ventures — if they can end-run the lobbying roadblock. "We regulate trade all the time," he said.

The bottom line: A large, complex regulatory world controls many aspects of the media business. Traditions of news have never prevailed, and will never prevail, on their own merits, even on the media frontier.

CHAPTER 7

Advertising: "Funny Money" and Other Issues

It began with Frozen Food Month, just another national sales promotion. But *The Arizona Republic* in Phoenix knew the food industry's "special" month could mean extra revenue. So it worked to get the dollars. The *Republic* put together a special advertorial section, sponsored by the food association, a local supermarket and the Coyotes professional hockey team, along with a contest that allowed 50 youngsters to spend an afternoon practicing with the pros. It was a veritable icefest in the Southwest desert, one that netted $100,000 in 1997, the first year, and $350,000 in 1999.

Convoluted? A bit. But more and more, this type of special promotion and partnership figures into the mix of media revenue still called advertising. These deals are not new, but as they proliferate they generate controversy. Journalists see the independence of news organizations tainted by the likes of, say, frozen food. At times, they might be right. In most cases, they're not.

At the heart of the matter is a change in media's commercial role. The old news-media triumvirate of consumer, advertiser and news producer is being reborn for the digital information world — with new tradeoffs, too:

• Readers and viewers no longer must consume news as soon as it is produced. They are gaining global access to information and commerce in an interactive new-media environment. It's a great advance in convenience and control, but the price may be some loss of community, privacy and journalistic independence.

• Advertisers will better target individual customers and niches but may have to give up on mass marketing.

• Media companies will have greater opportunities to form partnerships and to broker their relationships with all their customers — readers, viewers and advertisers. Consequently, some of these relationships will weaken or break.

DAILY NEWSPAPER REVENUE BY SOURCE (in millions)

Advertising

YEAR	RETAIL	NATIONAL	CLASSIFIED	TOTAL
1980	$8,609	$1,963	$4,222	$14,794
1985	13,443	3,352	8,394	25,189
1990	16,652	4,122	11,506	32,280
1995	18,099	4,251	13,742	36,092
2000	23,300	7,250	19,900	50,450

In short, opportunities and risks abound. All this affects the very definition of advertising, an industry that contributes 80% of newspaper revenue and virtually 100% of broadcast television receipts. Today, most of its rules and practices are up for grabs. For example, where do classified ads end and directory listings begin? Will image and brand advertising work in media that are usually devoted to selling specific goods? Will instant e-commerce — and the promotion and events that go with it — become a required element of advertising? How will sales forces get organized and trained for this complex, convergent world? Will technology provide new sales efficiencies? Will commerce overshadow news?

"The economic model is still evolving," said Louis A. Weil III, CEO of *Arizona Republic* parent Central Newspapers Inc. Weil believes regional or statewide newspapers with robust online services will emerge as the most powerful media serving U.S. consumers and advertisers, even in the digital age. Few, if any, newspapers have been more successful at it than the *Republic,* which teaches its sales techniques to other advertising directors.

"The editor is still king or queen," Weil said. Nonetheless, "someone has to put buyers and sellers together, and we are taking the opportunity to do that." The company has developed its sales force to be ready to deliver in many forms: online, in specialty publications, in newspapers and more, Weil said. "We've invested in the technology to do it right, and it's getting cheaper."

The shifting ad landscape

Advertising is about a $200 billion annual industry. The pie grows almost every year, one notable exception being recession-plagued 1991. Revenues reached an all-time high in 1999, but the respective portions for print, television, cable, direct mail and now the Internet are changing.

Circulation			Total
WEEKDAY	SUNDAY	TOTAL	
$3,864	$1,606	$5,470	$20,264
5,234	2,426	7,660	32,849
5,190	3,604	8,794	41,074
6,007	3,713	9,720	45,812
6,694	4,062	10,756	61,206

Source: Veronis, Suhler & Associates, Wilkofsky Gruwn Associates, NAA

Newspapers historically command the largest share and still do, after ceding the advertising lead to television in 1996 but regaining it in 1998. For newspapers, most ad spending is local. The TV sales channel is mostly national, although local stations split the ad slots with the networks. Local spot advertising is television's fastest-growing category. Cable's sales are mostly national, although regional sales networks have allowed local advertisers to reach audiences.

Audiences for traditional media have shrunk over the last decade, yet daily newspapers and networks continue to command increased rates for fewer eyeballs. Whether this can go on is debatable. One of the many perverse features of this new media age is that a mass audience is still difficult to assemble. So mass has maintained value, even when it's less massive.

Investment banker Nancy B. Peretsman of Allen & Co. said she didn't foresee this period of revenue growth and audience decline. "It's in the nature of advertising sources to shift to how people spend time," she said. Yet that shift didn't happen for dailies or for television, which has lost at least one-third of its viewership in the last five years.

Will the bubble burst? Signs persist that change is under way, or at least that the market is in flux. As futurist Lawrence Wilkinson, now an executive with Oxygen Media, observed, "Big transitions come with big shocks to the systems." Television revenue softened somewhat in 1999. Most networks made up the slack by increasing the number of minutes allocated for commercials — now as high as 16 per hour, up from 11 a decade ago. The public has noticed and complained. The clicker is more active than ever.

The practice of raising rates but not audience can't go on forever. "We're beginning to see resistance to rate increases," said *Arizona Republic* Publisher John F. Oppedahl. Nick Cannistraro Jr., CEO of the National Newspaper

Network, the Newspaper Association of America's ad-sales service, agreed. "We can't get growth out of rates anymore. We're pricing ourselves out of the market."

Unable to command higher rates, media have had to find new ways to attract more advertising. This requires a closer look at exactly how the ad business works. Advertising traditionally sells specific merchandise at particular times in a manufacturing cycle. Marketing dollars support this cycle. For example, advertisers allocate some money to distributors to give out discount coupons or create in-store displays. Manufacturers keep some ad dollars for themselves to spend at strategic times in a cooperative agreement with local retailers — hence the term "co-op advertising." Large retailers often advertise time-based discounts such as white sales, holiday sales or pre-pre-Christmas shopping.

Altogether, a finely honed machine spurs public tastes for particular products. It has worked especially well for media companies, which have gotten smarter over the years about getting the most out of each sales cycle — thus the frozen-food promotion in Phoenix, which drew upon the food brokers' calendar of events.

Newspapers, especially, follow the dollars by adapting to advertisers' business practices. They began zoned editions as suburbs grew. This practice gave readers more local news, but it also helped advertisers reach their target audiences more cheaply. Local cable operators are following suit, clustering their franchises to dominate the larger markets, then zoning advertising and sometimes news.

Some media, primarily newspapers, have entered the direct-mail business. This allows a media company to "own" a market, delivering advertising to everyone, including nonsubscribers. Free home-delivered or mailed publications have grown dramatically in the last two decades. Many large advertisers prefer slick, free-standing circulars to in-paper ads, although improved printing processes have added revenue for newspapers. *The New York Times'* adoption of color printing in mid-1997 garnered $6.3 million more in revenue from color premiums that year alone. Free-standing newspaper inserts continue to be a dominant financial force, however, bringing in three times the total sales of traditional network television.

AVERAGE AD RATE FOR 30-SECOND PRIME-TIME COMMERCIAL
(per 1,000 viewers)

1960	1970	1980	1990	1999
$1.70	$2.20	$4.80	$8.76	$12.00

Source: TV Dimensions 1999

Newspapers and TV networks face the same problem: seeking more revenue for smaller audiences. The practice of raising rates but not audience can't go on forever.

Some newspapers have sophisticated databases to more closely identify likely customers for specific advertisers. An advertiser can then market by neighborhood, census tract, ZIP code or postal route. Media companies do not sell these customer lists but massage their own data to manage distribution for the advertiser, much as a direct-marketing company would.

Also on this continuum is the special newspaper section, often tied to a sports or cultural event or an advertising cycle — the start of the football season, spring cleaning or gardening, for example. Practices vary, but some editorial departments develop the copy independent of the advertising department.

Occasionally, newspapers partner with civic institutions on the sections, not without occasional controversy. The recent advertising revenue-sharing deal between the Staples Center sports arena and the *Los Angeles Times* — referred to previously in Chapter 3 — brought a huge outcry from *Times* journalists, who protested that this practice had damaged the newspaper's credibility. Foremer executives, Times Mirror CEO Mark H. Willes, *Times* Publisher Kathryn Downing and Editor Michael Parks, ultimately apologized. More typically, the parties avoid conflicts of interest by signing cross-promotional contracts, paying each other in cash for specific amounts of ad linage or stadium signage. Indeed, the *Times* had already agreed, as a "founding partner" of the Staples Center, to pay the arena $1.6 million a year for five years for signage and rights to sell the *Times* inside, the newspaper reported.

More conventionally, media companies sponsor joint events with advertisers. A popular food writer, for example, might be the draw for a holiday entertainment "fair." A department or linen store provides the table settings; a local florist, table arrangements.

Cable networks are following suit, working with local operators and advertisers or community groups with events and contests: BET (Black Entertainment Network) sponsors "Personal Best Awards," a scholarship program co-sponsored by local businesses for teen-agers nominated by local affiliates. The Bravo network created a theater, dinner and shopping contest to promote its Broadway on Bravo program. ESPN, the sports network, sponsors a contest for a trip to an NFL training camp. These and numerous other promotional events produce millions of additional advertising dollars for local cable operators.

For decades, then, print media have found ways to grow revenue by being more than just a messenger announcing that Merchant X has goods for sale. Cable followed suit. Now, the Internet promises to further change the system.

Stated simply, the digital age speeds up business. Bar codes improve inventory control and warehousing. Computers enable consumers to book travel without travel agents. Futurists call this collapse of business functions "disintermediation." Get rid of the middleman. As the name suggests, media are the ultimate middlemen. And while they can never go away, their role will change in the new information age. It has to.

An example: Once consumers spot a deal, they immediately want to buy. Just knowing the goods are available is no longer enough. Interactivity rules. The digital revolution puts at issue:

• Historic advertising relationships between media companies, advertisers and consumers.
• The evolution of classified advertising.
• Media companies and their own e-commerce.

The morphing Internet ad puzzle

Advertising still moves goods and sells services, but the Internet is changing the what and how of it dramatically. Clearly, businesses can target potential customers more discretely online than in broadcast or in print. Advertisers will pay premiums for reliable niche audiences, so the new environment could support niche revenue flow at the expense of mass appeals.

Enormous effort, therefore, is going into shrinking the mass audience for advertisers. Nirvana in this realm is one advertiser's ability to sell one product to one consumer — a tantalizing proposition, though seemingly far in the future.

The opportunity to target customers online comes from two sources, both electronic. The best source is registration for, or purchases on, a Web site. A bit less useful is tracking people's Web-browsing histories, thus their interests, through their clicking patterns. The tracking devices are small files called "cookies," which businesses surreptitiously place in Internet users' computer systems while they are online.

The New York Times' online edition, registering more than 5 million customers, is gaining premiums from its advertisers. About 70% of Times users agree to receive targeted ads based on demographic information from the registration form and site-usage patterns. Similarly, amazon.com can talk directly to its customer base because it has a history of purchases and a knowledge of tastes. If you bought John Grisham's last novel, you'll probably get an e-mail announcing the latest book by Scott Turow, another writer of legal thrillers. The same principles apply to music compact-disc sales.

Will electronic marketing work as well for toys, drugs and everything else? That's unclear. The portal Excite.com encourages but doesn't require user registration. But it knows that users who personalize a home page on the site are five times likelier than others to be regular users. That's bankable with advertisers.

More difficult is gleaning likely buyers of products through "cookie" analysis. Theoretically, the technology exists to do this, but it is imprecise and expensive. Microsoft's Firefly service, built on a process known as "collaborative filtering," finds it difficult to sort clicking habits beyond a few characteristics such as geography or gender. This doesn't do much more than traditional direct marketing — identifying and selling to broad niches.

Though the Internet advertising business is a work in progress, online ad networks are pushing hard to figure it out and move the market closer to its electronic marketing potential. The biggest and boldest player here is DoubleClick, which claims to routinely measure 9,000 sites, representing the Web activities of half of all Internet users, to develop profiles of shopping habits. That knowledge helps businesses purchase Internet advertising. It's a tall order, described by General Manager Wenda Harris Millard as "delivering millions of customers, one at a time." Mostly, it identifies groups, narrowing but not eliminating the mass. To move closer to that one-on-one promise, DoubleClick has acquired new technology companies to build up its electronic sorting capabilities. But its potential for actually reaching its goal pro-

> **Given the seemingly infinite number of Web sites,
> it is taking the advertising world time to develop
> a sales network to actually place online ads on
> sites used by potential customers.**

duced public outcry and caused DoubleClick to move less aggressively.

Locating likely customers is only a piece of the Internet advertising puzzle. Sellers still have to reach them through banner advertising or Web-site sponsorship. Given the seemingly infinite number of Web sites, it is taking the advertising world a long time to develop a sales network for placing ads on sites used by potential customers. Many companies and ad agencies were slow to develop Internet units. Meanwhile, big portals got the business by default, an unsatisfactory solution to many sellers of goods and services.

"Yahoo! was getting 20,000 to 30,000 applications a day from potential advertisers," Silicon Valley advertising expert Janet M. Ryan said about the environment before online ad networks developed. Needless to say, Yahoo! and others in the same situation could process only a fraction of the requests. At the same time, Ryan said, "There was massive oversupply of Web banner inventory. Only 25% of that inventory was being sold." What sites were available, selling which audiences, and with what promise of sales return? Who knew?

This lack of an Internet sales infrastructure has delayed Web profitability, but as the new online ad networks meet Web sites' needs, a new tier of opportunities will come into play.

Large companies on the Web have put their own sales forces to work, analyzing usage patterns, then calling on manufacturers, retailers, service providers or ad agencies to sell banners or sponsorships. The iVillage portal targets women, so its demographic sell is fairly straightforward. Similarly, an ESPN or Dow Jones site also focuses on discrete subjects or audiences. For others, though, a good advertising fit has been problematic. That's where the advertising networks enter the picture.

DoubleClick and its biggest competitor, 24/7, will help big commercial entities, regardless of whether those companies sell directly to potential advertisers. Next down on the ad-network food chain is FlyCast, with about

100 smaller member sites, often lacking recognizable brand names and sales forces. FlyCast helps advertisers solicit information from Web users via surveys and the like, and it is beefing up its analysis technology.

Recently, networks have bought up "remnant" banner inventory and auctioned it to potential advertisers, much as airlines do for unsold seats close to flight time. Ad Flight and Ad Outlet are among the early providers, especially helpful to small Web-site owners. Remnant ad purchases are a low-cost way for otherwise traditional advertisers to supplement their sales efforts within identified niches.

Internet ad rates: the "cost-per-click"

Once the Internet advertising pathways are built, the next challenge becomes what to sell on the Web. The question may seem silly, but it is a real issue for sellers. Do you sell merchandise or brand? The answer appears to be: some of both.

That wasn't so clear in the beginning, said DoubleClick's Millard. "Now, most people understand that it's a hybrid ad medium."

Traditional media, especially newspapers, have problems using their sales forces to sign up online advertisers. Print advertising reps are used to packaging short-term, high-volume sales opportunities for big retailers such as department stores, food stores and car dealerships. The object is to move wares. But smaller and specialty merchants, like some online merchants, need a different plan. They mostly want small branding ads that run periodically to seed their products into the public's awareness. Dailies' failure to meet these needs in the past fostered the growth of city magazines and alternative weeklies.

What will happen next in the online sales environment is still in the realm of crystal-ball gazers. The trick for news-media Web sites will be to accommodate both direct-sale and conceptual ads.

Pricing will be an important part of the equation. In 1999, Internet advertising revenue ranged between $1.75 and $3 billion, depending on who's measuring. Big advertisers always seek the least costly, most efficient means to reach a target audience. Traditional media developed customer profiles to help advertisers decide which programs or publications to buy. Similarly, general user profiles allowed individual Web sites to command 1999 rates between $5 and $25 per 1,000 users.

More importantly, this interactive environment can perform one feat advertisers have tried to accomplish for years: figuring out exactly how many people saw an ad and shopped. Retailers have used surveys, coupons, contests and many other devices to measure advertising effectiveness. Sales volume proved that advertising worked, but businesses did not easily know if they were overpaying or if one medium or company was superior to another.

On the Internet, they know exactly how many Web users click on an ad. Rates increasingly reflect this measurement, much as TV or newspaper rates are adjusted if viewers or readers don't match the promised volume. Procter & Gamble, Macy's and Gateway computers all advertise based on cost-per-click pricing. Placing an ad is no longer an act of faith.

The cold classified facts

Classifieds are the heart and soul of print advertising, earning newspapers $18.6 billion in 1999, about 40% of all newspaper advertising revenue. Every new entrant into the media business wants classified advertising — Microsoft, phone companies and a host of other Internet purveyors. Their market-making ads touch the common denominators of American financial life: employment, housing and automobiles. In the face of Internet competition, newspapers are scrambling to keep this shining pot of gold.

But one thing is clear about the Internet: Its database technology, searchability and interactivity make it a more natural business environment for classified ads. In the print world, advertisers rarely market more than 10% of their car or home inventory. On the Internet, they can list everything, at a lower cost and often without media middlemen. Buyers can find what they want quickly and precisely, without trawling pages and columns of listings. In the late-century, full-employment economy, the Internet is gaining favor with employers and job seekers alike.

The shift has hurt ad sales in a number of cities, including Los Angeles, San Jose, Calif., Chicago and Dallas. A.H. Belo Corp., which owns *The Dallas Morning News,* has seen its stock price go into a prolonged depression, which some analysts attribute to the drop in classified revenue. However, this linage has begun to increase recently as many employers find they need both print and online advertising to reach job seekers.

Almost all newspapers with Web sites post their classifieds. Some charge extra for it, some don't. The industry is learning, however, that posting ads alone buys little competitive relief. Static listings in an interactive medium don't fly. The national-local split also comes into play. Traffic is heavy on the large national sites, but they'll need local agents or affiliates as more people transact business online. Who will those partners be?

Although 1999 sales were higher, automakers and dealers sell about 15 million vehicles each year. At an average price of $22,650 per vehicle, this sector represents a $340 billion business. Because of rules governing franchise operations, 22,600 local dealers manage the actual sales. Forrester Research Inc. estimates that each dealer spends about $18,750 a month on external advertising, or $335 per vehicle sold. Just over 60% of dealers maintain Web sites, which cost an average $250 a month to maintain — less than the mar-

Shopping online is one thing. Buying is another. If the name of the game is to control the customer relationship, increasingly that means getting involved in the sale, a new and complicated role for news-media companies.

keting cost supporting one vehicle sale. In 1998, 2 million car buyers used the Internet at some stage in the process. That number is expected to grow by 2003 to more than 8 million, more than half of all purchases.

How will these cold, hard facts change advertising practices?

Traditionally, television builds brand awareness for new cars and announces urgent financial offers, such as sales, rebates or special financing arrangements. Newspapers point readers to individual dealers for new or used cars with special model-by-model prices; they also provide a marketplace for individuals selling cars. Now, many of these listings end up on the Internet, sometimes tied to newspaper advertising, sometimes not.

Among the top five auto-listing Web sites, the largest is CarPoint.com, owned by Microsoft. Also in the top tier is Cars.com, a service of Classified Ventures, eight newspaper-owning companies' joint project to gain national scale in classified advertising as they also build out local market opportunities. Individuals can list cars directly on the service or through a participating newspaper. Cars.com offers dealers a host of services, including inventory updates, Web workshops or even Internet site development. It also directs buyers to dealers by ZIP code. CarPoint, on the other hand, does not solicit listings directly online. It finds specific vehicles from its network of affiliated dealers. It shares additional information on Web sites, often including consumer reviews and blue-book values.

Online recruitment advertising also is branching out from the print model. More and more, newspapers are hosting job fairs — online and at live events — providing résumé and other services to job seekers and advertisers alike. In 1999, The Washington Post Co., Tribune Co. of Chicago and the venture capital firm of Accel Partners formed a partnership called Brass Ring Inc. that will offer a host of job training and employment-related services for prospective employees.

E-commerce advances marketing synergies

The Internet invites action — moving a sale to closure. Credible product and merchant information, the old stuff of advertising, is nice but not enough. Shopping online is one thing. Buying is another. If the name of the game is to control the customer relationship, increasingly that means getting involved in the sale, a new and complicated role for news-media companies. E-commerce produced about $18 billion in sales in 1999 and is projected to nearly double to $33 billion this year and grow to $108 billion in 2003. Sales figures are huge, but profits have yet to materialize in most cases.

In the past, media enterprises have focused on "core" businesses central to their publishing, advertising or programming missions. In the early days of television, networks owned programs and do again after recent deregulation. For years, newspapers have owned newsprint companies to ensure supplies. As the classified market began to change in the late 1980s, some media companies purchased car-auction businesses, in part to ensure access to used-car listings and sales. More recently, they have purchased whole or partial stakes in sports teams to ensure access to local sporting events for their TV stations and cable networks. Sports programming draws young adult males, and large cable networks such as ESPN, MSG (Madison Square Garden sports) and the Fox regional sports networks have bought exclusive broadcast rights. Local broadcasters responded by buying the teams, thus controlling the terms and revenue from these rights.

The Internet corollary for this is e-commerce. Don't just advertise a car. Direct potential buyers to a dealer, a financing company, an insurance broker — collecting advertising and transaction fees from each along the way. CarPoint has such an arrangement with General Motors, and Cars.com with Ford Motor Co. and with the Yahoo! and Go Network portals, the latter a Disney venture.

The real estate segment offers similar opportunities. Don't just list houses or apartments; collect fees for connections to sales agents and financing companies. Just as in the automotive category, national real estate networks are springing up. Microsoft Network offers this kind of one-stop shopping via its HomeAdvisor service, and real estate agents post their own listings on Realtor.com, the largest residential and commercial property site.

These sites do more than list properties. They include information and vendors for financing, insurance and renovation — all the players to close a real-estate deal. The newspaper consortium Classified Ventures has three sites: Apartments.com, Home Hunter.com and NewHomeNetwork.com, and each offers services beyond listings. Realtors and newspapers, once business partners, are suddenly competitors with more complex relationships.

Cable companies, via cable modems, also are looking to the promise of e-commerce. Why the rush? Because apart from advertising, online transactions promise fees, much as a bank's ATM assesses a fee for doing business.

On the Internet, these activities can be measured so that payment is based on actual usage. That's the good news. The looming issue for news-media companies is institutional credibility. Will a skeptical public believe that journalism remains independent from the company's marketing relationships? They seem to with America Online and other portals. How can the companies ensure enough degrees of separation? At *The Arizona Republic* the mantra is, "We know the difference between advertising and news."

Cookies and spam: not just for eating anymore

If companies can follow our "cookies" all over the Internet, then privacy becomes a bigger concern than ever for consumers and news organizations. In the absence of site registration or e-commerce, cookie-tracking technology usually cannot target single users for advertising. But it can detect general demographic information — which, in turn, can bring unwanted e-mail advertising, also called "spam."

"There's a difference between commerce sites and content sites and the expectation of users," said Kathy Lynn Cullotta, a Chicago-based consultant who advises companies on sales strategies. "There's just a different trust relationship with sites when you're looking for information and when you're buying. 'Do you want fries too?' does not offend when you're already making purchases, but it's a different experience when you want information."

In that spirit, most news-media sites ask permission to send sales-related e-mail when they register users. The MSNBC site steers clear of direct commercial solicitation based solely on users' Internet browsing patterns. As Microsoft executive Steven J. White put it, such behavior adds a "creepy factor" that consumers reject. It's a matter of enlightened self-restraint. Many other sites, but not all, do the same.

What could slow down the Internet's roaring growh? Widespread "cyber-scam," said inventor Jaron Lanier, who coined the term "virtual reality." All the commercial efforts under way make that a real possibility. The public may be equally serious about privacy. The smart will tread carefully.

The bottom line: The Internet's closer nexus between information and commerce entangles journalists and marketers in different relationships than they have had in traditional media. As news-media companies develop an array of new marketing and advertising practices, they will need to negotiate new standards and write new rules to compete in the digital information age both profitably and honorably.

CHAPTER 8

Implications: Putting It Together

Rust Belt vs. Sun Belt. That was The Debate of the 1970s. Industrial manufacturing moved from older cities, mostly in the North and East, to newer, growing communities, mostly in the South and West. But the shift represented more than a geographic change. It reflected a whole new way of thinking and doing business, a shift from old assets to new ones. It often left tradition locked in the old institutions but not fully adopted by the new — unionization, for example. Many older communities adapted to the shift and revived. Many didn't and foundered.

For a new generation, the shifting future of news mirrors that era of change. The outlook is complex, mixing old and new, rusty old presses and spanking new computers, struggling maturity and booming growth. The most senior journalists in the oldest news institutions lament newspaper and network newsroom cutbacks at a time when investment in news is actually growing in many news organizations. Quality? Forget it, they say. It's all down the tubes. But do their complaints reflect reality — or the difficulty of coping with change in the information age? Increasingly, it looks to be the latter.

Change is painful. Between 1989 and 1991, the years of greatest financial stress on newspapers, the editorship of almost every major daily newspaper changed hands, sometimes the result of mandatory retirement, but mostly not. Those who came of age in the industrial world of news found the new technological and financial constrictions too difficult to manage. All big-three broadcast TV networks changed presidents since this study began in 1997, when pressure on broadcast profitability took hold anew. One develops a rhythm of work. When the financial or organizing assumptions change, the job changes as well. Old dogs are reluctant to learn new tricks, and hefty company stock portfolios make doing so less necessary.

Today's changes are not hard just on those in the news media. They're difficult for anyone trying to create, use or understand information. Why?

Managing change is really hard.

Several years ago, before the World Wide Web burst onto the scene, the big hype concerned 500 channels on cable TV. Like a lot of hype, this contained a grain of truth: Three broadcast stations per market in 1950 had grown to an average of 45 broadcast and cable channels by 1996. Anyone was to have any amount of programming at any time. That hasn't happened, at least not yet, because marketplace realities once again have trumped theory. Broadband Internet connections and digital-TV systems have become more important investments. But the vision ran into other problems, too.

A 500-channel world is tantalizing in the abstract, but the human attention span may be more finite. In a 20-channel world, most people juggle programs on 10 to 12 channels on a regular basis. In a 50-channel world, people still can manage only 12 regular channels. Will the same be true for regular Web-site usage? No one has measured this yet, but the principle is firmly in place: Infinite choice does not equal infinite activity.

Moreover, change can fool companies that try to stay on the cutting edge. Is bold or cautious better? Being the first with a product or service is great, when the timing is just right and the pioneering company catches a new wave and rides it. CNN was first to market with 24-hour international news. *The Wall Street Journal* caught the business-news wave years ago. *USA TODAY* caught two waves — the TV-generation reader and the business traveler. Amazon.com is trying the same for Internet retailing.

But being first can be bad if you're too far ahead. In the 1980s, Knight Ridder sunk tens of millions of dollars into its Viewtron videotex project, to provide electronic news and shopping information. It never took hold. Again, in the 1990s, Knight Ridder supported its executive Roger F. Fidler's vision of a handheld, flat-panel device — an E-paper prototype, retaining a news-paper's look and portability. Again, it was too much too soon.

Time Warner, too, tried hard to develop an on-demand TV service in Orlando, Fla. That also flopped. The company then built a less ambitious and very successful interactive cable service, offering entertainment and regional news, in partnership with *The Orlando Sentinel*.

The daring failures made traditional news companies wary. In 1997, for example, at least three public news-media companies each generated more than $500 million in cash flow with no real plan to spend the money for strategic advantage. The trend continued. Buy cable. Sell cable. That option's now closed through consolidation. Make a big acquisition. But which one? Which next big thing could make a difference? The prices were so high that every investment seemed like speculation. Mostly, the money went toward repurchasing company stock, paying down debt or developing a modest Internet presence.

"There is a difference between preparing for what's ahead and forecasting.

> Change can fool companies that try to stay on the cutting edge. Is bold or cautious better? Being the first with a product or service is great, when the timing is just right and the pioneering company catches a new wave and rides it. ... But being first can be bad if you're too far ahead.

We're not forecasting," said Washington Post Co. CEO Donald E. Graham about his company's attitude and approach to change. Instead, the Post Co. chose to solidify its local base, affiliate with national news operations and leverage its Kaplan education subsidiary into training and recruitment services related to classified advertising.

There are a few bold actors, but most companies hedge. Partnerships, however, are forming among media and Internet companies, lowering the financial risk of new ventures. More news-media companies are joining the game, finally, as a result.

Desperately seeking "new" news

Copyright and other intellectual-property laws exist to encourage the creation of new ideas. The creators' rights can be used or sold. But in the industrial world of news, this protection favors distributors and producers over content providers. Facts can't be copyrighted. Competitive advantage lasts only one news cycle. This morning's investigative story is old news by tonight. And most news organizations belong to The Associated Press, which has a contractual right to use the information in a member's story after it has appeared. Resellers of news, especially those with proprietary delivery systems like America Online, have an advantage over the initial publishers.

In the past, big news organizations provided national and international coverage to small communities via news services. The balance is changing in the Internet world. Portals, the largest content providers, have no reporting staffs. One of the most competitive online battles involves the portals' selection of wire services. Reuters and United Press International (UPI) are in a footrace with the AP to be the provider of choice.

In this environment, where is the incentive to gather and deliver fresh information — "new" news? This study began with just that question in

> **Some answers are emerging from companies with strong brand recognition. They are cutting deals and forming partnerships to extend their brands to other media and collect revenue for supplying content.**

mind. In the new Internet world, where is the incentive to create important public-service stories — not stock prices or sports scores but enterprise reporting of oft-delayed value?

Clearly, people want and need to know about government corruption, financial fraud or environmental pollution. But how will this reporting be manifested in the new media environment? Original, civic-based reporting will continue to draw audiences to traditional media. But what happens if a big piece of the advertising pie flows away from the information creators and toward the packagers? Who would pay for such coverage then?

Could investigative reporting services spring up, for example, developing their own brands and selling to Internet sites as new-age news syndicators? This would not be without precedent. I.F. Stone was an influential independent. Seymour M. Hersh broke the story of U.S. military atrocities in the Vietnam village of My Lai for the tiny Dispatch News Service. A few tenacious journalists or entrepreneurs might find this a successful model. However, it does not on its face offer a reliable enough revenue stream to ensure systematic and vigorous reporting of civic concern.

Some answers are emerging from companies with strong brand recognition. They are cutting deals and forming partnerships to extend their brands to other media and collect revenue for supplying content.

Most simply, attempts to have consumers pay for content on proprietary sites did not work. But consumers have been willing to pay for stories from news archives. Almost all large news companies charge for material archived on the Internet after publication.

TV news programs, too, are formally teaming up with newspaper reporters in "co-branding" relationships. Among the new partnerships:

• *The Washington Post* and *Newsweek* have an exclusive contract for their reporters to appear on MSNBC cable news programs.

• *The Wall Street Journal* has a similar partnership with CNBC and a joint venture with NBC for overseas news broadcasts.

• Salon magazine signed on as content developer for Rainbow Communications, including the Bravo cable channel.

Synergistic arrangements also help companies reduce the cost of enterprise reporting by using it in multiple media, each of which can sell advertising. Time Warner's "NewsStand" series, a collaboration between four of its magazines and CNN, is one such effort. *The New York Times* uses customer knowledge from its registered Web users to charge premium rates for Web-site advertising. To extend the brand further across media, it has made several efforts to develop TV programs, some more successful than others. Joint newspaper, broadcast, cable-TV and Internet news operations in Dallas and Chicago are potentially the most profitable and efficient. The federal ban on newspapers' local cross-media ownership prevents replication in all but a few cities, but the ban is under challenge.

And, of course, the future ability of traditional local news providers to serve as gateways or portals — to be that first screen a consumer sees — will go a long way toward settling these economic issues in their favor.

A hunger for authenticity

An even more basic concern, amid all the media consolidation, will be the need for authentic voices to counteract the Greek chorus of conventional wisdom that is commodity news. This is what younger people yearn for when they hear archaic and superior authorities telling, but not showing, them the news.

Rainbow Communications moved toward developing its new brand voice by investing in Salon.

Much more will be required, though. Media historian Mitchell Stephens of New York University believes that scholars and media executives need to develop a whole new visual "language" — grammar, syntax and all — to tell stories in the 21st century, much as video games have done with sound and color to signal the presence of an "enemy."

Business consultant David Sibbet of San Francisco-based Grove Consultants International takes this further. Having analyzed organization and communication within hundreds of nonprofit and high-tech companies around the world for more than 20 years, Sibbet believes news businesses unknowingly work against their basic interests.

Based on the research about young adults' busy lives, many news purveyors respond by shortening their reports for easier skimming and scanning. While this serves busy newspaper readers, Sibbet said, the information still has to be deep enough to connect with the reader, creating an emotional bond and loyalty to the storyteller. In other words, short stories may titillate but longer stories can resonate.

His thinking dovetails with one ad agency's study of young people's attitudes toward the media. The firm, BBDO, found that respondents felt the greatest affinity with magazines, whose long-story form engendered trust.

Stephens and Sibbet might both be correct. Electronic media might develop increasingly visual systems that navigate through information to the trusted interpretation underneath. The question is whether traditional news companies will lean toward navigation or interpretation, or can they learn to embrace both?

In the vastness of cyberspace, it is difficult to hear a single voice. But if news organizations with civic traditions are to survive, their digital voices must be distinct. Useful information is good. But Internet sites also must create a "buzz." It's easy to confuse buzz with sensation. They are not the same. The issue is the quality of conversation, and news providers must learn new things to say.

Ownership vs. leadership

For more than a quarter of a century, the bad rap on the news industry was that it had moved from family to corporate ownership, giving up public interest for profit. Industrial giant ITT backed away from its attempts to acquire the ABC television network in the late 1960s because of public concern that business interests would influence the news. It took until 1985 for regulatory fervor to recede sufficiently to allow General Electric to purchase RCA, owner of the NBC network, and for Loews Corp. to acquire CBS. That same year, Capital Cities Communications bought ABC, but CapCities/ABC was a media company, not an industrial behemoth. During the same period, media critic Ben Bagdikian wrote screeds challenging "chain" ownership of newspapers. He claimed it destroyed news coverage.

The world was more complicated than that. True, many corporate owners assigned new editors or publishers to communities — executives that did not know them as well as home-grown talent did. Their coverage sometimes revealed a tin ear for critical community issues. But they often invested more resources in coverage, and business practices improved to ensure the future health of the franchise. On the whole, it is difficult to argue convincingly that journalism of the 1990s is inferior to the family brands of the 1960s.

Another wave of complaint came when numerous family companies went public or at least sold public stakes in their companies. The newsroom sometimes felt immediate and frivolous effects. At *The New York Times,* for example, corporate cost-cutting required an assistant managing editor's signature to obtain a back copy of the newspaper.

At the same time, the most prestigious family-owned institutions created classes of stock or large employee or foundation stakes that allowed incumbent owners to maintain control. Among them: The New York Times Co., The Washington Post Co., Dow Jones & Co., The Times Mirror Co. and A.H Belo Corp. Such arrangements sometimes fail to prevent turmoil related to finance or control, especially if the family members chose to sell or change management so they can earn more. This happened at Dow Jones and Times Mirror, which recently sold to Tribune Co. The fact is that family financial needs can be as unforgiving as those of the general marketplace.

Ownership pressure on the journalistic process becomes a more important issue as corporations with numerous business interests take over news-media companies. What happens when the corporation itself is the subject of news? Time Warner's board of directors mandated editorial independence in coverage of the corporation, said Time Inc. Editor in Chief Norman Pearlstine. Despite similar policies at many other public media companies, journalists and media critics remain suspicious.

Perhaps a more important way to assess performance of news companies is to look not only at ownership but at leadership. Little is written about this topic, even though so much about news leadership is changing in this fast-paced era of the 24-hour news cycle.

A key leadership challenge concerns the speeded-up time frame in which decisions must be made, said Merrill Brown, editor of MSNBC.com. The need for moment-to-moment decision-making is even more intense on the Internet than at the wire services. Newspaper or TV-news editors have less control than they used to, when they could more thoughtfully package stories and feeds. In a 24-hour cycle, no one fully shapes the news in the way that, say, Ben Bradlee did during his tenure at *The Washington Post*. The system and cycle is too big for any one leader.

Another aspect of leadership concerns editorial independence. Journalists who came of age in the 1960s and 1970s were less concerned about this, as most of their CEOs came from the newsroom. At Gannett Co., The Washington Post Co., Knight Ridder, Dow Jones & Co. and Scripps Howard, the top executives and many newspaper publishers had been journalists first, business leaders later. Now, corporate leadership is reverting to those from the finance and marketing fields, historically a more typical pattern of media company leadership. The old questions of church and state now form the crux of today's news leadership battles.

No one has been more closely identified with the corporatization of news than Gene Roberts, former prize-winning editor of *The Philadelphia Inquirer* and retired managing editor of *The New York Times*. Roberts' departure from Philadelphia was contentious. Publicly, the conflict was framed as the editor vs. the bean counters, but Roberts rejected that characterization. Rather, he said, his departure was about institutional values usually worked out in a budget process.

"In the past, everyone came with their wish list, and we hammered it out," Roberts said. Eventually, he was expected to come to budget discussions with cuts in place. "We never got to talk about what we'd like to do — what we thought was necessary to do," he said. "That was important because often there were surplus funds, and we could use those to pay for stories or series that did not make their way into the final budget."

The big showdown over journalistic independence and investment is yet to come. These are good times. In the cyclical news business, an austerity cycle will reappear — as it did when this inquiry began. The much-discussed idea of permanent prosperity is unrealistic, said investment banker Herbert Allen. "Markets get tired," he noted.

The bottom of the business cycle, demanding sharper choices, will determine the true value of news in the digital age.

Where is the journalistic leadership?

Journalists discuss the future of news a great deal. Not so across the business divide. The American Society of Newspaper Editors has collaborated with the business-side group, the Newspaper Association of America, on readership issues — but not about the traditions of news. This research project attempted, but failed, to engage TV news directors and station managers in a discussion about news quality.

The Freedom Forum and the Pew Foundation are among those trying to ignite a crucial debate about news-media credibility and processes. In 1999 the Knight Foundation began an annual summit for the most senior media-business executives to discuss news values.

Reporters can continue to report, staying aggressively ignorant about the business of news. But those willing to engage may find opportunities to effect change. It's not about protest, per se. As "60 Minutes" commentator Andy Rooney said concerning "The Insider," the recent movie about CBS honchos who quashed a "60 Minutes" story about tobacco-industry abuses, "There are only so many times you can quit."

Only education and action will carry the day. Associations can engage the process. Individual journalists can learn about the economics of news. Reporters and editors have never been happy with news as it was produced in real time; they always wanted to make it better. How can they do so now?

Individual companies offer examples of journalistic leadership. Somewhat ironically, among those working hardest to inculcate journalistic values into their institutions are the same companies working most aggressively on new advertising, promotion and e-commerce plans: for example, *The Arizona Republic* in Phoenix and *The Orange County* (Calif.) *Register*. Editors Pam S.

> The big showdown over journalistic independence
> and investment is yet to come. These are good times.
> In the cyclical news business, an austerity cycle will
> reappear. ... The bottom of the business cycle,
> demanding sharper choices, will determine the true
> value of news in the digital age.

Johnson in Phoenix and Tonnie Katz in Santa Ana spend a great deal of time and money "teaching" — explaining institutional change, setting goals and helping editorial staffs refine a journalistic mission in a much changed world.

Michael Fancher of *The Seattle Times* is another editor guiding his news staff to think about decision-making and institutional values, as well as writing and editing. Editors have organized and run *The Hartford* (Conn.) *Courant's* companywide leadership program. Frank Sutherland of *The Tennessean* in Nashville uses its crusading publisher emeritus, John Seigenthaler, as a mentor to the news staffs, tying old values to new practices.

The California-based Maynard Institute for Journalism Education conducts newspaper Total Community Coverage programs. Using cultural diversity as the prism for change, TCC jointly trains editorial and commercial departments on how to succeed in competitive and fractured media markets.

Sometimes, crisis indeed brings opportunity. In the wake of the Staples Center controversy at the *Los Angeles Times,* reporters and editors there are developing a program to teach journalistic principles to business-side executives.

But why wait for controversy before assuming such institutional leadership? The moment has come for others to follow suit. Journalists who feel whipped about by their changing world have many opportunities to help shape that world. The reality of Web-based information means that a growing number of editorial employees have technical skills but little or no background in the processes and traditions of news. Who will teach them? Who will ensure that what's good about the old world of news makes its way into the new?

Company Profiles

Who gives us the news? Who doesn't? In the converged media world, news comes compliments of any number of companies.

Media businesses have been among the most enduring franchises in America, having been built on the monopoly power of the industrial media age. But this is the digital age, and much about the economic structure of success is up for grabs. Individualism gives way to partnerships. So far, however, media companies generally have not succeeded in collaborations.

Old ways persist. But many new ways emerge. The local information market grows into the regional distribution hub, almost like FedEx. The phone company buys wire-service news and sends headlines over your beeper. Cable channels and broadcast networks package newsmagazines for airport or airplane. Resort hotels pass out faxed news summaries as beach fare. E-mail messages replace "snail mail." In many ways, any information company is in the news business today, but only a few dozen are key in shaping its future. We chose 16 for this study, which became 13 through mergers by the end of 1999.

The selection was difficult and excludes some players with important strategic operations. Time and resources shortened the list. Among the obvious omissions are Bloomberg L.P., the financial-news conglomerate that was among the first to develop a digital, multimedia information management system and to figure out what to sell and what to give away; Advance Publications Inc., owned by the Newhouse family — the nation's fourth-largest newspaper company, with 23 dailies that reach nearly 3 million readers, and a major magazine dynasty, Condé Nast Publications Inc.; and Cox Enterprises Inc. of Atlanta, which publishes 16 newspapers and operates cable systems.

In addition, there are numerous privately held, regional newspaper and broadcasting groups, some of which the report cites. The Reuters and Agence France-Presse news services are major international for-profit competitors of The Associated Press. Public television and radio share many of the audience

135

and programming problems faced by commercial broadcasters. Radio broadcasters provide vast amounts of news, although little of it is original. An infinite number of Internet operations cater to niche audiences in a way reminiscent of earlier times.

Altogether, however, the following companies account for most attempts to cope with changes in technology, styles of news consumption and revenue sources.

What might the list look like five years from now?

ABC (Disney)

History

ABC, formerly the American Broadcasting Co., is one of the original "Big Three" radio and television networks. In 1966 industrial giant ITT bid to become the first nonmedia company to acquire a network. The FCC rejected the sale following public protests that such ownership risked commercial contamination of the news. ABC merged with Capital Cities Communications Inc. in 1985.

In 1995 CapCities/ABC Inc. was acquired by the Walt Disney Co., an entertainment company with film, theme park and resort, cable, sports, music, home video and book interests.

Third in the Nielsen ratings for years, ABC News grew in stature and audience share under the leadership of Roone Arledge, who added "Nightline" and "This Week with David Brinkley" to the lineup.

By the Numbers

- Owns 10 local TV stations, reaching 24% of the U.S. viewing audience, in addition to the ABC network and cable channels. Disney's 30 radio stations reach an estimated 14 million listeners.
- Employs 1,800 journalists and technical workers in 23 ABC News bureaus worldwide.
- Invested a reported $11 million for ABC's 24-hour New Year's millennium coverage, making an estimated profit of $5 million.

REVENUES/OPERATING INCOME

Fiscal year ended September 30, 1999

	Disney Co. $	change	Broadcast Networks $	change	Cable Network $	change
Revenue	23.4b	2%	4.6b	(1%)	2.8b	17%
Operating income	3.2b	(21%)	656m	(33%)	952m	24%
Net income	1.4b	(27%)				

Source: Walt Disney Co.

Strategy

Disney did not fully absorb CapCities/ABC until 1998. Its corporate emphasis is on growth of its entertainment units, including cable. It sold the former CapCities newspapers to Knight Ridder and sold many of its consumer magazines as well. Network news represents a decreasing share of business operations.

ABC's news quality is high overall, but its ratings sometimes suffer from heated competition. And its growth is constrained by lack of cable distribution. "World News Tonight" competes head-to-head with the "NBC Nightly News." The network's news division changed strategy in 1998, giving up individual program fiefdoms to consolidate production resources. "Nightline" remains an exception.

"20/20" absorbed "Prime Time Live" and gained an expanded schedule. The network invested heavily in a new Times Square studio for "Good Morning America." Meanwhile, Sunday morning policy gabfest "This Week" has declined.

ABC joined CBS and Fox to form a new video news service. Its Internet activities are growing but compete with other news providers for exclusive portal services. Veteran correspondent Sam Donaldson has left prime-time television to host an Internet-only Webcast, "SamDonaldson@ABCnews.com."

ABC News President David Westin has aggressively pushed investment in high-impact programs like the millennium coverage. More recent projects generated controversy over news standards.

Business Mix

ABC is a unit within a newly formed Media Networks division for Disney's broadcast, cable and Internet interests, including:
- The ABC television and radio networks plus owned and operated local TV stations.
- Major stakes in numerous cable networks, including the ESPN sports networks, the Disney Channel, Lifetime, A&E and the History Channel.
- Television syndication.
- Investments in Internet ventures, including Yahoo! and the Go Network.

....

PETER E. MURPHY
Senior Executive Vice President and Chief Strategic Officer,
Walt Disney Co.

On the role of news at Disney: "Our strategy is to reach consumers 24 hours a day with a full-service network. Part of taking a full-service offering to consumers is having news."

America Online Inc./
Time Warner Inc.

History

In January 2000, America Online (AOL), the nation's largest online information company and Internet Service Provider (ISP), announced a merger with
Time Warner Inc., the largest media company.

AOL was founded in 1985 and went public in 1992. It has survived and
prospered, despite numerous business and financial setbacks, earning itself the
name, "cockroach of the online world." During its expansion, it acquired
Netscape, which developed the first commercial Internet browser, and Movie-
Fone, the film-ticketing service.

Time Warner Inc. resulted from the 1990 merger of Time Inc., the publishing empire founded by Henry Luce, and the Warner Bros. film studio and
cable behemoth. It acquired Turner Broadcasting, including the Cable News
Network (CNN), in 1996.

By the Numbers

• Will exceed $30 billion in combined 2000 revenues — $5 billion from AOL,
  $26.8 billion from Time Warner.

AMERICA ONLINE REVENUE/OPERATING INCOME (in millions)

| | Year ended June 30 | |
	1999	1998
Subscription Services Revenue	$3,321	$2,183
Advertising, Commerce and Other Revenue	1,000	543
Enterprise Solutions Revenue	456	365
Total revenue	**$4,777**	**$3,091**
Operating Income*	**$578**	**$66**
Net income*	**$396**	**$59**

* on a fully taxed basis before one-time changes

Source: America Online

- Jointly employs 82,000 workers.
- Reaches one-third of U.S. households through combined media.
- CNN:
  - Reaches more than one billion people in 212 countries and territories.
  - Operates 34 international news bureaus, employing 3,500 news professionals worldwide.
  - Has invested more than $1 billion in its international channel group.
  - Has contracts with more than 600 local broadcast stations for "first film" usage.
  - Owns 1,600 radio affiliates.
- Time Inc.:
  - Receives 25% of all U.S. magazine advertising revenues.
  - Reaches 90 million magazine readers.
- AOL:
  - Serves nearly 22 million subscribers worldwide.
  - Is the largest online-news provider, with four services ranking in the top five.
- Time Warner Cable:
  - Operates the second-largest system in the U.S., with 12.6 million subscribers.
  - Serves 180,000 customers through its cable modem Internet service, Road Runner.

Strategy

The AOL-Time Warner merger would create a totally converged media company with deep content offerings across media and distribution platforms. Before the merger announcement, AOL faced competition that limited access to

TIME WARNER INC. REVENUE/OPERATING INCOME (in millions)

	Nine months ended September 30	
Revenue	**1999**	**1998**
Cable Networks	$4,425	$3,985
Publishing	3,327	3,160
Music	2,616	2,731
Filmed Entertainment	5,688	5,790
Broadcasting — The WB Network	246	170
Cable	3,968	4,015
Intersegment elimination	(835)	(874)
Total revenue	**$19,345**	**$18,977**

Source: Time Warner Inc.

broadband services. The merger combines two subscriber-based distribution systems, marketing data for advertisers, and financial resources unavailable to most free Internet sites or broadcast networks.

News would be available online, on cable TV and in weekly magazines. CNN and Time Inc. magazines have joint programming. Time Inc. abandoned its attempt to group popular magazine titles on the Internet under the Pathfinder brand. Its cable systems are clustered in major markets. AOL's "community building" strategies include active online efforts to increase voting, especially among Internet-savvy young adults.

CNN has video service contracts with numerous U.S. local broadcast stations but has no sister broadcast network. Time Warner produces local cable all-news programming in some of its major markets, including New York City.

Business Mix
- AOL's online services, including CompuServe.
- Time Warner's cable systems, networks (HBO, CNN and Turner channels) and partnerships.
  - Warner Bros. studios, feature films, theaters, television and retail stores.
  - Music publishing and recording.
  - Sports team ownership.
  - Magazine publishing, including *People, Time, Fortune, Sports Illustrated, Money* and *Entertainment Weekly.*
    - Book publishing and book clubs.

STEVEN M. CASE
Chairman and CEO, America Online Inc.

On making the deal work: "We had to learn about the traditions of Time Warner, about the traditions of Henry Luce. It's not just about making money. It's also about serving the public interest."

On the nature of online news: "This medium provides an expanded sense of the value of news to people's lives. They are consuming news and information more — and more diligently. Before, they were happy to have their news delivered once or twice a day on their doorstep. Now, they want to use it, connect with it, delve into it, share it with others, and most important, manage it. Today's consumer wants news in-depth, in real time, just as Wall Street and Washington get it."

W. THOMAS JOHNSON
Chairman, CNN News Group

On journalistic mission: "News organizations — anchors, correspondents, producers — must be independent of special interests. Free to report the truth. Free to pursue investigative journalism. Free to expose corruption, wrongdoing, ethical misbehavior. Supported by owners who will not permit damage to their most important assets, their reputation. Without public trust in our news coverage, we will lose the respect of our viewers, our readers, our listeners, our advertisers, our subscribers."

The Associated Press

History

Established in 1848 by six New York City newspapers cooperating to reduce the cost of gathering news from Europe. The Associated Press leased wires for transmission in 1875. It incorporated in 1900 as a nonprofit cooperative in New York state and opened membership to "all qualified newspapers" in 1943.

The AP began supplying radio stations in 1933 and then television. It established a radio news network in 1974. In 1994 the cooperative launched a newsroom system for TV stations (NewsCenter) and created APTV, an international video news service. That same year it also purchased competitor WTN (World Television News) from a European consortium to consolidate and expand. In 1997 it launched the Electronic News Production System, first for the British Broadcasting Service and later for U.S. broadcasters.

By the Numbers

- Distributes news and photos to more than 8,500 outlets worldwide.
- Serves 5,000 U.S. radio and TV stations and 1,700 U.S. newspapers.
- Operates 95 bureaus in 67 countries and 145 U.S. bureaus.
- Serves subscribers in 112 countries.
- Employs 3,500 people, with personnel costs consuming half of its $550 million budget.
- Transmits 20 million words and 1,000 photos daily.
- Has won 45 Pulitzer Prizes, 27 for photography.

REVENUE/EXPENSES (in millions)

	1999	1998	1997
Revenue	$550	$494	$441
Expenses		$496	$449
Loss before tax benefit		(2.1)	(7.2)
Net loss		(1.6)	(4.8)

Source: The Associated Press

Strategy

The AP's challenge of a decade ago: how to grow the news service, maintaining public-interest coverage without pricing itself out of business. The answer came in a suite of new for-profit ventures that leverage AP's sophisticated technology and a distribution system that reaches every newsroom in the world. One-third of its revenues now come from these ventures, which subsidize coverage. Newspaper revenues now makes up less than half of the total.

The AP maintains a bureau in each U.S. state capital even as fewer news organizations have a statehouse presence. It created and helped newspapers finance electronic photo processing, allowing instantaneous transmission and greatly reducing costs. New online businesses, including video services, are a big revenue source. The trick of successful ventures: immediate positive cash flow *and* enhancing members' products instead of competing with them.

Business Mix

- A worldwide nonprofit news cooperative for print and broadcast.
- Photographic distribution services and a new photo archive.
- An electronic advertising-transmission business, AD SEND, linking ad agencies with publications or Web sites.
- A business-news partnership with Dow Jones, AP-DJ.
- AP Interactive multimedia services department that provides wire news, photographs, and video design and content to Web sites and manages Internet initiatives.
- APTV, an international news video service based in London, and a sports-news counterpart, SPTV.
- An all-news radio service.
- An electronic news production system designed for the BBC and globally marketed to news providers.

PATRICK T. O'BRIEN
Senior Vice President/CFO, The Associated Press

On AP's decision to develop television services: "We were looking at our product for gaps. Although the world had become more visual and multimedia, we didn't have a video product. It's become more important than it was when we built APTV (in 1994). Now online and newspaper members can put up text and photos on a Web site with video and sound."

A.H. Belo Corp.

History

Alfred Horatio Belo founded the company in 1865 from a partial interest he bought in the publisher of the *Galveston* (Texas) *News*. He began publishing *The Dallas Morning News* in 1885 under the leadership of George Bannerman Dealey, a company executive. Dealey bought the *Morning News* from Belo's heirs in 1926 and named the company in Belo's honor. Dealey descendants still control the company, which went public in 1981. Its hometown *Dallas Morning News* won the war for regional newspaper dominance, and Belo has diversified into print, broadcast and cable TV under CEO Robert W. Decherd.

By the Numbers

- Generates $1.4 billion in annual net revenues.
- Publishes seven daily newspapers, including *The Dallas Morning News, The Providence* (R.I.) *Journal* and *The Press-Enterprise* in Riverside, Calif.
- Circulates 900,000 newspapers daily and 1.3 million on Sunday.
- Owns 16 TV stations, reaching 14% of U.S. households.
- Owns or has a stake in four regional all-news cable networks.

NET REVENUE/OPERATING INCOME (in millions)

		Full year 1998A	Full year 1999A	Full year 2000E
Net Revenue				
Broadcast TV		$609	$599	$695
Newspaper		787	817	857
Cable and other media, estimated		11	18	25
Total		**$1,407**	**$1,433**	**$1,577**
	% growth	13%	N/A	11%
Operating Income		**$233**	**$264**	**$306**

Source: Company reports and PaineWebber estimates

Strategy

Belo is constructing local and regional franchises across media, mostly in the Southwest and Pacific Northwest, and is leveraging properties into local online portals. After a year of lagging earnings, classified linage and stock price, the company has rebounded. It bolstered its television advertising revenue by exploiting increased time-slot allocation with affiliated networks.

The present focus is on convergence and building upon its reputation for high-quality news in print and on television.

The flagship Dallas newspaper and TV station form the nucleus of Belo's Texas Cable News service, which combines print, Internet and station resources in Austin, Houston and San Antonio. A similar channel operates in Seattle as North-West Cable News, drawing upon Web sites and reportage of four regional TV stations. The company has invested in satellite operator Geocast to use new digital broadcast spectrum for simultaneous, multimedia content distribution.

Business Mix

- Newspaper publishing.
- Television broadcasting.
- Belo Productions provides programming for its all-news regional cable stations in Arizona, Texas and the Pacific Northwest.
- A 12.4% stake in the Dallas Mavericks NBA franchise.

....

BURL OSBORNE
President/Publishing Division, A.H. Belo Corp.
Publisher, The Dallas Morning News

On perpetuating core values in a growing company: "Our value system was transmitted by osmosis for the first 100 years. Now, our management committee worked on a policy and concluded these five things are most important to reinforce: excellence, integrity, fairness, inclusiveness, sense of purpose."

On managing a group of newspapers: "We set the values and let the editors and publishers do their jobs. I monitor (agreed upon) financial results and intervene only if we have a problem. We operate on the theory that people closest to an audience and reader base are in the best position to manage. There's no cookie cutter. Each market and audience is different."

CBS (Viacom)

History

CBS, founded by broadcast pioneer William S. Paley, was known for years as the "Tiffany network" because of its high-quality programming. Edward R. Murrow and colleagues virtually created network television news after World War II. Longtime anchor Walter Cronkite was known as "the most trusted man in America." Laurence A. Tisch acquired the company in 1985, a year of corporate acquisition and cost-cutting at the "Big Three" television networks.

Broadcasting and industrial conglomerate Westinghouse bought CBS in 1995 and later Infinity Broadcasting, a radio group run by Mel Karmazin, who became the company's CEO and largest shareholder. Westinghouse sold its industrial assets in 1997 to focus on broadcasting. In two 1999 transactions, the company sold a minority stake in Infinity and announced a merger with entertainment giant Viacom, headed by Sumner Redstone. The deal is under regulatory review.

By the Numbers

- Generates combined revenues of $18.9 billion.
- Owns 33 TV stations, reaching more than 40% of U.S. households.
- Owns a majority stake in 163 Infinity radio stations.

REVENUES/OPERATING PROFIT [LOSS] (in millions)

	Revenues			Operating Profit (Loss)		
		Year ended December 31:				
	1998	1997	1996	1998	1997	1996
Radio	$1,893	$1,480	$554	$542	$372	$140
Television	4,373	3,589	3,372	138	119	189
Cable	546	302	191	50	10	40
Other	(7)	(4)	26	(248)	(248)	(315)
Total Continuing Operations	**$6,805**	**$5,367**	**$4,143**	**$482**	**$253**	**$54**

Source: Securities and Exchange Commission reports

- Owns more than 110,000 advertising billboards.
- Has full or partial interest in seven Web sites.

Strategy

After a decade of contraction under Tisch ownership, CBS began growing again in audience and profitability under Karmazin's leadership. It placed its advertising sales force on commission and tapped the promotional power of television, using advertising inventory as "virtual" currency in acquisitions and to promote CBS programs across media.

CBS' programming draws the oldest television viewers, averaging more than 50 years old, a demographic that supresses advertising rates. The network is trying to attract younger audiences, especially men, by reviving sports coverage; it paid an estimated $4 billion for NFL football rights. The merger with Viacom will increase content and distribution synergy.

CBS plans no net growth for news programming, opting to hold onto viewership with alternative, "deeper" approaches to stories and by investing in small-growth niches such as prime-time newsmagazines and morning programs. For instance, "60 Minutes," the granddaddy of newsmagazines, spawned the younger, hipper "60 Minutes II." As CBS shifts its resources from old programs to new ones, the overall news budget will see a small decrease. Seeking efficiencies through partnerships and collaboration, CBS joined the ABC and Fox networks in creating new video services for affiliates, pooling crews for major stories.

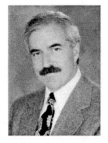

ANDREW HEYWARD
President, CBS News

On CBS News' philosophy: "We have a contract with the audience to provide fair, accurate, excellent reporting of worthwhile stories. Everything must meet that requirement. There are other requirements. The news division is a business and must attract an audience large enough to survive."

On the Tisch legacy: "It was obviously a period of missed opportunity. The emphasis was on short-term survival rather than long-term success. The failure to invest in a cable news network is a drawback. Now we have a longer view that supports success."

Business Mix

- Two broadcast networks, CBS and UPN, and their station groups.
- Infinity Broadcasting radio stations nationwide.
- Television production companies (programs include "Entertainment Tonight"), TV syndicator King World Productions and a majority stake in the Spelling Entertainment Group.
- Extensive cable holdings, including MTV, Nickelodeon, the Comedy Channel and The Nashville Network.
- Paramount Pictures, other film imprints, and movie theaters.
- Home-video businesses, including Blockbuster.
- Paramount theme parks.
- Numerous book publishers, including Simon and Schuster.
- Outdoor advertising.
- Internet ventures and alliances, including news services for America Online.

Dow Jones & Co.

History
Three reporters named Charles Dow, Edward Jones and Charles Bergstresser in 1882 created a daily financial newsletter delivered by messenger to subscribers on Wall Street. By 1889, the newsletter became *The Wall Street Journal,* delivered by telegraph. Clarence W. Barron bought the company in 1902 and expanded its financial-news offerings to include the *Barron's* weekly. After the Barron-Bancroft family bought the company in 1928, it retained control when the company went public in 1963 and, more recently, forced improvements in profitability. Dow Jones expanded into community newspaper publishing and financial business information services, some of which it has sold.

By the Numbers
- *The Wall Street Journal* is the second-largest U.S. newspaper, with average daily sales of 1.8 million.
- Employs a staff of 8,300 employees worldwide, including 650 newsroom professionals.
- Publishes 19 daily and 15 weekly newspapers through Ottaway Newspapers, acquired in 1970.

NET REVENUE/OPERATING INCOME (in millions)

		Full year 1998A	Full year 1999A	Full year 2000E
Net Revenue				
Advertising		$1,031	$1,255	$1,231
Information Services		670	326	406
Circulation & other		456	450	458
Total		**$2,157**	**$2,001**	**$2,094**
	% growth	(16%)	(7%)	7%
Operating Income		**$294**	**$389**	**$399**
	% margin	14%	19%	19%

Source: Company reports and PaineWebber estimates. PaineWebber figures are rounded.

- Dow Jones Interactive offers news and information from more than 6,000 sources, serving more than 350,000 online subscribers.

Strategy

Dow Jones is the dominant U.S. distributor of financial news and information to consumers and business professionals. The precision and timeliness required for the professional information market creates added-value products that consumers are willing to buy. Attempts to deliver real-time market data through the Telerate service and to own TV stations failed, and Dow Jones sold those properties in 1997 and 1998.

Future growth prospects are threefold: partnerships, overseas news wires and online extensions of its print products. Dow Jones Interactive is the largest paid-subscription service on the Internet, with a goal to double subscriptions in five years.

Business Mix

- *Wall Street Journal* editions in the U.S., Asia and Europe plus financial-news inserts in Latin American newspapers and weekly Sunday inserts in 10 U.S. newspapers.
- *Barron's,* the weekly business and financial weekly.
- The weekly *Far Eastern Economic Review.*
- Wall Street Journal Interactive and related online information services.
- Ottaway Newspapers Inc. of Campbell Hall, N.Y., publisher of dailies and weeklies nationwide.
- Factiva, a joint venture with Reuters Group PLC for business-based financial information.
- Content partnerships with the NBC network in CNBC in the U.S. (co-ownership of CNBC in Europe and Asia) and with The Associated Press.
- Dow Jones market indexes.

....

PETER R. KANN
Chairman and CEO, Dow Jones & Co.
Publisher, The Wall Street Journal

On strong editorials and separation from news operations: "The only alternative lies in the fashionable argument that there are no basic values of right or wrong, that news is merely a matter of views, that truth is only in the eye of the beholder. Or the notion, which prevails elsewhere, that journalism is merely another tool for the pursuit of partisan or ideological — or commercial — objectives."

Gannett Co.

History

Frank E. Gannett and a partner bought an interest in the Elmira, N.Y., newspaper in 1906; expanded their holdings; moved the headquarters to Rochester, N.Y., in 1918, and continued building a media empire. In 1947, CEO Paul Miller took over a company with 21 newspapers and seven radio stations. He continued the expansion and launched *FLORIDA TODAY* in 1966 to coincide with the growth of the U.S. space program in Cocoa Beach. Gannett Co. went public in 1967. Allen H. Neuharth became CEO in 1973, acquired small newspaper groups, and merged with Combined Communications in 1979, adding significant broadcast and outdoor-advertising holdings. Gannett launched *USA TODAY* in 1982, relying heavily on satellite transmission and upgraded color printing. It later acquired (and divested) the cable holdings of Multimedia Inc. In 1999, the company purchased Newsquest PLC in England.

By the Numbers

- Publishes 74 daily U.S. newspapers, including *USA TODAY*.
- Sells about 6 million newspapers a day, including *USA TODAY*'s 1.8 million.

NET REVENUE/OPERATING INCOME (in millions)

		Full year 1998A	Full year 1999E	Full year 2000E
Net Revenue				
Newspaper & other		$4,159	$4,456	$5,052
Television net revenue		721	724	779
Cable		241	261	0
Net Revenue		**$5,121**	**$5,441**	**$5,831**
	% growth	8%	6%	7%
Operating Income		**$1,444**	**$1,619**	**$1,753**
	% margin	28%	30%	30%

Source: Company reports and PaineWebber estimates. PaineWebber figures are rounded.

- Newsquest publishes 11 newspapers in England, with daily circulation of about 450,000.
- Owns and operates 21 local TV stations, reaching 17% of U.S. households, primarily in mid-size markets.
- Employs a workforce of 45,000 — 45% women, 27% minorities.
- *USA TODAY* alone employs 420 in the newsroom, 100 in its online service and 20 abroad.

Strategy

After decades of diversifying its holdings, Gannett is mostly consolidating its newspaper and TV operations in mid-size markets — returning to its local roots, but with scale. Corporate marketing and technology departments support the whole system. In the past three years, the company sold its radio stations, outdoor-advertising business, and is in the process of selling its remaining cable operations. It has clustered newspapers in some markets and sold more than a dozen others.

A current goal is to develop its holdings into local Internet portals. In all but a few cases, it is sitting out full Web-site development, letting big-market media operators — with their bigger audiences and revenue potential — struggle through the shakeout while competition is at its fiercest. In the interim, Gannett uses its national product and brand, *USA TODAY*, to its audience-building and financial advantage while developing technological expertise and partnerships.

Business Mix

- Flagship *USA TODAY, USA TODAY* magazine, *USA TODAY* Baseball Weekly and the *USA TODAY* Information Network.
- Gannett News Service and 74 daily newspapers nationwide.
- Army Times Publishing Co., including the *Army Times, Navy Times, Air Force Times, Federal Times, Defense News* and *Space News*.
- Television stations.
  - Marketing services.
  - Offset printing facilities.

....

THOMAS CURLEY
President and Publisher, USA TODAY

On *USA TODAY*'s birth: "You couldn't start *USA TODAY* today because there is not the excess press capacity in the U.S. we had in 1982. There's competition now for press sites."

Knight Ridder

History

Knight Ridder was formed from the 1974 merger of Knight Newspapers Inc. and Ridder Publications Inc. Charles L. Knight purchased the *Akron* (Ohio) *Beacon Journal* in 1903. When he died in 1933, the newspaper passed to sons John and Jim, who assembled a newspaper group including dailies in Miami, Detroit, Chicago and Philadelphia. Knight Newspapers went public in 1969.

Ridder Publications began in 1892 when Herman Ridder purchased a New York City, German-language newspaper. Its early acquisitions included *The Journal of Commerce* in New York City and two St. Paul, Minn., newspapers. The Ridder group included smaller-city dailies such as those in Duluth, Minn., Long Beach, Calif., Gary, Ind., Boulder, Colo., and Wichita, Kan., and a few large dailies, such as the San Jose, Calif., *Mercury* and *News*. Ridder Publications also took its stock public in 1969.

In the 1980s Knight Ridder launched and folded Viewtron, the nation's first full-scale consumer videotex service. As it continued to expand its news-

NET REVENUE/OPERATING INCOME (in millions)

		Full year 1998A	Full year 1999E	Full year 2000E
Net Revenue				
Retail advertising		$1,089	$1,114	$1,155
General advertising		262	306	324
Classified advertising		1,012	1,037	1,052
Circulation net revenue		588	586	593
Other media revenue		142	178	231
Total		**$3,093**	**$3,221**	**$3,355**
	% growth	7%	4%	4%
Operating Income		**$505**	**$627**	**$656**
	% margin	16%	19%	20%

Source: Company reports and PaineWebber estimates.

P. ANTHONY RIDDER
Chairman and CEO, Knight Ridder

On Knight Ridder's mission: "Knight Ridder Corporation is a newspaper company that delivers quality information in both print and electronic form. We feel we have a special obligation — because of the kind of business we are in — to serve our communities with fair, honest, objective journalism that people can trust."

On the rebound in recruitment classified advertising: "Companies like Cisco, Yahoo! and E*Trade are advertising for employees with us. They have told us that the Web, while important, is not effective in isolation. It generates neither the number nor the quality of leads they need — particularly in terms of passive job seekers. We do."

paper group, the company gained a reputation for high-quality reporting. It acquired and later sold TV stations and cable interests as well as proprietary research and business information services. It invested in, but later suspended, development of a portable electronic newspaper. In 1997 it acquired the former CapCities newspapers from the Walt Disney Co. and sold or swapped several others. The next year Knight Ridder moved its headquarters from Miami to San Jose, Calif. — the heart of Silicon Valley.

By the Numbers
- Publishes 31 dailies in 28 markets, the second-largest U.S. newspaper group in terms of circulation.
- Has a combined paid circulation of about 4 million daily, with a readership of 9 million daily and 13 million Sunday.
- Employs 22,000 workers, including 5,400 in editorial and 400 online.
- Operates 15 overseas bureaus.
- Supports 45 local Web sites via the Real Cities portal network.
- Helps 1,250 community groups create their own Web pages and calendars, with growth exceeding 50 organizations a week.
- Generated $18 million in 1998 Internet revenue and $32 million in 1999.
- Doubled its operating income margin, now 20%, between 1995 and 1999.

Strategy

After nearly two decades of diversification strategies involving broadcasting, business information services and technology ventures, Knight Ridder has returned to its roots as a newspaper company. Its largest footprint is in the San Francisco Bay area with two major dailies plus community weeklies, all connected on the Internet by BayArea.com. The corporate goal is to marry online services to the dailies, emerging as community information portals — then to build a national network of regional hubs under the Real Cities co-brand. Nongroup papers in Dallas, Phoenix and Minneapolis have joined.

For most of this decade, Knight Ridder battled depressed earnings in Rust Belt markets by cutting costs — incurring labor problems and criticism from journalists as a result. It moved the corporate headquarters to San Jose, Calif., to change its culture to one embracing the Internet and to be closer to new technology and ventures. As an early adopter of online services, the company created KnightRidder.com as a separate business unit to manage Internet operations. Current distribution partners include America Online, Digital Cities, *USA TODAY* and CNN.

Economic and demographic changes in local markets remain a management challenge. Classified advertising in San Jose rebounded in 1999 after a sharp falloff year in 1998, a cycle that other major dailies have shared. The company has created foreign-language newspapers and Web sites: Spanish in Miami, Spanish and Vietnamese in San Jose.

Business Mix

- Daily newspapers in 18 states.
- Community weekly publications in Miami, Philadelphia and San Francisco's East Bay plus other suburban newspapers.
- New-media subsidiaries and partnerships.
- Partial stakes in The Seattle Times Co., Fort Wayne (Ind.) Newspapers Inc., Knight-Ridder/Tribune Information Services, retail- and classified-ad sales networks, and newsprint companies.

NBC (General Electric)

History

The National Broadcasting Co. (NBC) has been a unit of diversified industrial giant GE since 1985. NBC began in the 1920s as one of two radio networks developed by General David Sarnoff, head of RCA. RCA set up networks to build up music programming and thus its radio sales. As the NBC radio and television networks developed, they established a long tradition of cultural and public-service programming in the era of heavy broadcast regulation and limited competition. RCA diversified but later sold its car rental, book publishing, real estate brokerage and other holdings. The GE takeover brought cost-cutting, business management and controversy to NBC and its news division. Later strategies brought ratings success, profit and growth of news programming through cable and online ventures.

By the Numbers

- Owns and operates 13 TV stations, reaching 28% of U.S. households.
- Reaches 60 million homes with the MSNBC cable network.
- Expects MSNBC to break even in 2000, based on larger audiences, increased advertising revenue and more cable operators carrying the channel.
- Employs 1,500 at NBC News, including 600 at the network, 350 at MSNBC cable (exclusive of the Web site), 400 at CNBC and 100 at the affiliate services center in Charlotte, N.C.
- Spends $120 million on its news payroll: $90 million for the network, $30 million for cable.

REVENUES/PROFIT (in billions)

	Full year		% increase
	1999	1998	
Revenues	$5.86	$5.27	11
Profit	1.6	1.35	18.5

Source: General Electric

Strategy

Arguably, NBC has been the only profitable broadcast network in the recent past. It differs from rival networks, all of which have co-owned movie studios, in that it relies more heavily on "nonfiction" programming than on sports and entertainment. The network expanded its prime-time newsmagazine schedule more extensively than its competitors and sat out the football bidding war, keeping college and professional basketball, golf, tennis, horse and car racing, and the Olympics.

News and entertainment programming targets younger women and commands premium ad rates as a result, even for smaller audiences in some cases. "Today" is No. 1 in morning television. NBC is quietly renegotiating compensation payments to affiliates to reduce network programming costs.

A cable entrant and early adopter of new technologies, NBC created a partnership with Microsoft to support cable and online news services, each of which was No. 1 among news providers in its medium in 1999. The network's multiple channels and platforms create news-distribution efficiency and economy, allowing "cutting and pasting all over the place." Its latest focus is on exclusive content partnerships, Internet portals (national and local) and e-commerce. When NBC launched the publicly traded NBC Internet (NBCi) in 1999, it created a property that could bring content, search capabilities, online communities, shopping, direct marketing and e-business services under one roof.

Business Mix

- The NBC television network and local broadcast affiliates.
- Cable news programming on MSNBC (with Microsoft) and CNBC (with Dow Jones).
- Additional cable partnerships, including the History Channel, A&E and Rainbow Media Holdings.
- Internet ventures include the top-ranked news site MSNBC.com, NBCi (linking Snap.com and other portals) and investments in 14 other companies.
- A minority stake in Paxson Communications (72 stations and the Pax cable network).

ANDREW LACK
President, NBC News

On competition, generally: "We made a bet that if in the next century there is only one 24-hour news provider, it must be us. Why shouldn't it be us?"

News Corp. (Fox)

History

News Corp. grew from Chairman and CEO Rupert Murdoch's Australia-based holdings into a global media enterprise spanning 70 countries. Murdoch started out with the *Adelaide News,* inherited in 1953 from his father, newspaper executive Keith Murdoch. With this single property as a base, the younger Murdoch started a national newspaper, *The Australian;* and bought *The* (London) *Times, The Sunday Times* and some London tabloids. He went on to acquire newspapers, television networks, magazines, book publishers and satellite networks around the world but primarily in the United

SALES REVENUE/OPERATING INCOME (in millions)

Sales revenue	1999	1998
Filmed entertainment	$7,078	$5,897
Television	6,161	4,865
Magazines and inserts	2,228	2493
Newspapers	4,134	3,773
Book publishing	1,224	1,087
Other	949	834
Total	$21,774	$18,949
Operating income		
Filmed entertainment	$553	$375
Television	879	930
Magazines and inserts	543	586
Newspapers	689	669
Book publishing	77	55
Other	11	31
Consolidated Operating Income	$2,752	$2,646
Operating profit before income tax and outside equity interests	1,373	1,950

Source: News Corp.

States, where one of News Corp.'s crown jewels is Twentieth Century Fox.

Murdoch survived several challenges to his U.S. media ownership as a foreign national by becoming a U.S. citizen and making business alliances with his foes. He narrowly escaped bankruptcy in 1990. Always a controversial media figure, critics often accuse Murdoch of using his media empire to advance business or political agendas usually labeled "conservative."

News Corp.'s 1999 annual report trumpeted the theme, "Around the World, Around the Clock," and the multimedia conglomerate calls itself, "the only vertically integrated media company on a global scale."

By the Numbers

- Posted fiscal 1999 revenues of $21.8 billion, 74% from U.S. operations.
- Employs 50,000 worldwide, with the Fox News Channel employing 800 full-time and 100 as free-lancers (about 650 at the New York City headquarters and 130 in the Washington, D.C., Los Angeles, London, and Hong Kong bureaus.
- Owns 22 local Fox Broadcasting Co. stations, reaching 40% of U.S. households, with stations in nine of the 10 largest markets.
- Holds broadcast rights to 3,500 live sporting events, covering 73 of the 76 professional U.S. sports teams.
- Serves 41 million cable homes with the Fox News Channel, for which Fox pays cable operators $10 per subscriber.

Strategy

Around the world, News Corp. has extensive newspaper holdings and satellite interests, working systematically to expand media markets in Europe and Asia.

Over two decades, it has shifted its U.S. operations from newspaper publishing to diversified entertainment assets in broadcasting, movies, sports and ancillary ventures that support them, aimed primarily at young viewers.

....

ROGER AILES
President, Fox News Channel

On criticism by media critics that Fox is ideologically conservative: "We said we were going to do fair and balanced news, and that scared them. We were adding points of view. That's the reason we got into this business. The issue is not bias. It's arrogance. Many believe that God created them to shove their points of view down the public's throat. There's no tolerance for other points of view."

Fox.com is an e-commerce site connected to Fox television. News Corp. owns one U.S. newspaper, the *New York Post,* which it acquired under a waiver of the newspaper-broadcast cross-ownership rule, and broadcasts some breaking stories from its newsroom.

The company continues to build its news assets. The Fox News Channel provides a unique, more conservative voice on all-news television and is gaining prime-time viewership with commentator/host Bill O'Reilly. Meanwhile, the broadcast network strengthens its local Fox stations by requiring affiliates to produce local news programs, acknowledged builders of audience and advertising revenue. These programs strengthen an infrastructure combining a national broadcast network and a 24-hour cable news network. Only NBC already has such a system. Fox has joined ABC and CBS in a new video service to provide footage for major events and to pool resources to cover them. Its partnerships with broadband providers will expand high-speed Internet connections to homes, delivering Fox news, sports and entertainment content in new formats with increased interactivity.

Business Mix
- Ten broadcast, cable and satellite channels, five in the U.S.
- Regional sports networks in major U.S. cities, sports teams and related entertainment enterprises.
- Twentieth Century Fox, Fox studios and other filmed-entertainment subsidiaries.
- Book publishing, including HarperCollins.
- Newspaper publishing, mostly in Australia and Great Britain, including *The Times* of London.
- Magazine publishing, including *TV Guide.*
- News America Digital Publishing, a new online unit.

The New York Times Co.

History

Adolph S. Ochs bought the flagship *New York Times* in 1896. For four generations, the family retained control of the newspaper and the company, which went public in 1968. *The New York Times* has won numerous First Amendment battles over the years and now focuses on leveraging its brand as the "best newspaper" in the U.S across media. The *Times* added color in 1997.

NET REVENUE/OPERATING INCOME (in millions)

	Full year 1998A	Full year 1999E	Full year 2000E
Net Revenue			
Newspaper	$2,642	$2,802	$2,986
New ventures/Times Co. Digital	23	27	39
Broadcast	151	155	175
Magazine group	121	118	120
Total	**$2,937**	**$3,102**	**$3,321**
% growth	2%	6%	7%
Operating Income by unit			
Newspaper	$491	$641	$773
New ventures/Digital	(13)	(23)	(30)
Broadcast	45	57	76
Magazine	22	27	30
Corporate cash expenses	(30)	(31)	(34)
Depreciation & amortization		(105)	(187)
Total operating income	**$515**	**$566**	**$628**
% margin	18%	18%	19%

Source: Company reports and PaineWebber estimates.

By the Numbers

- Publishes 23 newspapers, including *The Boston Globe.*
- *The New York Times:*
  - Is the third-largest U.S. daily, with 1.1 million paid circulation and 1.7 million Sunday, 40% of which circulates outside the New York metro area.
  - Penetrates about 12% of New York metro-area households.
  - Serves 159 markets, with 50% of sales from home delivery.
  - Contributes 55% of Times Co. revenues.
  - Employs 1,150 on editorial staff.
  - Has won 79 Pulitzer Prizes.
- Owns 8 TV stations, reaching about 4% of U.S. viewers.
- Owns New York radio stations and three golf magazines.
- Times Company Digital encompasses 50 Web sites, including *The New York Times* site, with 10 million unique viewers, 60% of whom don't read the newspaper.

Strategy

After various attempts at diversification over the years, including magazine publishing, the Times Co. has a three-pronged approach to business growth. First, build *The New York Times* brand nationally and across as many media as possible, including TV production and the Internet. Second, build loyalty among its high-demographic audience and extract revenues from related businesses such as credit cards, memberships and events. Third, manage regional and local print and broadcast properties as high-margin contributors.

To sharpen that strategic focus, the company recently decided to sell seven

ARTHUR SULZBERGER JR.
Chairman, The New York Times Co.
Publisher, The New York Times

On the Internet and the *Times:* "At the core of *The New York Times'* offerings is our news report and the quality and trust that it engenders, but an Internet-based community will need more than that to sustain itself. In addition to quality news and quality advertising, we must offer quality communication and quality e-commerce.

"To do so, we will create a Quality Network, a kind of 'knowledge portal' where users of the Web can come to get the best information from *Times* journalists, from 'outside' experts and, perhaps most importantly, from each other."

smaller-market newspapers plus nine of its telephone directories. The move allows greater concentration on larger newspapers, such as the *Worcester* (Mass.) *Telegram & Gazette*, which the Times Co. recently acquired. The Worcester daily, the third largest in Massachusetts, will contribute to synergies with *The Boston Globe*. By design, the New York Times Regional Newspaper Group's higher margins help fund the company's larger national strategy.

Times Co. Digital, through the *New York Times* site with its registered users, provides marketing data unavailable to sponsors of open, free sites. This data should help yield advertising premiums and marketing opportunities. Among the other Web sites from Times Co. properties: *The Boston Globe's* regional portal, Boston.com; WineToday.com from *The Press Democrat* in Santa Rosa, Calif.; and NYToday.com, a regional entertainment portal.

All these efforts fit within a global "Quality Network" of Web sites the Times Co. is developing. Using a model resembling network television, it has "owned and operated" sites from its newspaper, magazine and broadcast properties and affiliated partnerships with other information providers. It supports each large company-sponsored site with sophisticated technology to allow individual users to develop communities of interest. Unlike most other new-media entrants, it is accounting for the costs of providing Web content, reimbursing newspapers for the content they provide and paying them for the advertising they sell.

The Times Co.'s overall strategy is to build on industry growth trends nationwide and reduce reliance on classified advertising. It also wants to increase *The New York Times'* daily circulation by 250,000 in 10 years. The company's Business Information Services division resells newspaper content to online information providers.

Business Mix
- Metro, regional and community newspapers.
- Television and radio broadcasting.
- Golf magazines.
- Business information services.
- Times Co. Digital, now going public as a separate company, managing all online services.
- Investments and joint ventures include a $15 million investment in TheStreet.com; minority stakes in two newsprint companies; and joint ownership (with The Washington Post Co.) of the *International Herald Tribune,* which circulates 228,000 copies daily in Europe, Asia and Israel.

Tribune Co. (plus Times Mirror)

In March 2000, Tribune Co. of Chicago announced it would acquire The Times Mirror Co. of Los Angeles for approximately $8 billion in cash, stock and debt assumption. The deal would make Tribune the third-largest newspaper publisher and one of the largest broadcasters in the United States.

The Acquisition
Tribune and Times Mirror together would create:
- The only media company with a TV station and newspaper in the three largest media markets — New York, Los Angeles, Chicago — and in Hartford, Conn.
- The third-largest newspaper company in circulation, approaching 4 million.
- The owner of seven newspapers in the top 30 markets and 10 television stations in the top 12 markets.
- The largest local market provider of interactive services.

Tribune Co.
History
The Tribune Co. of Chicago was one of the first big-city newspaper publishers and radio/TV broadcasters in the U.S. The company grew around the

JOHN W. MADIGAN
CEO, Tribune Co.

On the deal: "By joining together, we are building a national 'footprint' for our company with size, scale and scope to stay competitive in a rapidly consolidating marketplace. The merger also provides the platform to expand our local interactive business into a truly national presence...and will compare favorably with competitors such as *The Wall Street Journal, USA TODAY* and *The New York Times.*"

Chicago Tribune, founded in 1847 and bought by Joseph Medill in 1855. His grandson, Col. Robert R. McCormick, ultimately inherited the *Tribune* and became its best-known editor and publisher as well as a controversial figure in American press and politics. His cousin Joseph Medill Patterson, who edited the *Tribune* from 1910 to 1925, founded the New York *Daily News* in 1919, which along with newsprint mills, radio (1921) and television (1948) also came under the Tribune Co. umbrella.

Over the years, the business mix changed. The company sold the *Daily News* and its California newspapers, some after contentious labor actions. In the last decade, the company expanded its broadcast holdings substantially; started two 24-hour regional cable news channels; sold its newsprint interests; and created an education publishing unit. It has invested heavily in technology and the Internet.

By the Numbers
- Generates more than $3 billion in net revenues.
- Owns 23 TV stations, reaching 27% of U.S. households; superchannel WGN; two all-news regional cable networks; and 25% of the WB network.
- Publishes four daily newspapers.
- Operates four radio stations.
- Employs more than 13,400 workers, about 90% of whom own company stock.
- Generates $20 million (1999) in revenue from Internet sites.
- Stores 10,000 résumés in its BlackVoices.com job data bank.
- Reaches 92,000 subscribers with a magazine guide to football at historically black colleges.

Strategy
Before the acquisition, Tribune developed a diversified media company that built strong and convergent local media franchises into national brands with

NET REVENUE/OPERATING INCOME (in millions)

		Full year 1998A	Full year 1999E	Full year 2000E
Net Revenue				
Broadcasting & entertainment		$1,153	$1,294	$1,386
Publishing		1,499	1,569	1,621
Education & other		329	374	388
Total		$2,981	$3,237	$3,395
	% growth	10%	9%	5%
Operating Income		$702	$782	$852

Source: Company reports and PaineWebber estimates.

heavy reliance on new technology. Its holdings are broad and deep in news, entertainment and educational products. Its large broadcast group consists mostly of WB or Fox affiliates reaching younger television audiences.

To advance contingent news operations, it developed a joint broadcast-print Washington bureau to serve all company outlets. Its Chicago news operation brings *Tribune* reporting to television and radio, as well as to ChicagoLand Television, an all-news cable channel. Its other 24-hour cable channel, Central Florida News 13 in Orlando, is a joint venture with Time Warner, providing zoned, regional coverage.

As part of an active Internet strategy, Tribune Co. invested early in America Online, Excite@Home, Digital Cities and iVillage. It is a founder and partner of two newspaper Internet classified advertising consortia, Classified Ventures and CareerPath.

The Times Mirror acquisition extends Tribune's strategy of building a national network of traditional and new-media businesses by consolidating operations in the largest local media markets. The deal also challenges federal cross-ownership restrictions.

Business Mix

- Broadcast: Local TV stations with WB or Fox affiliation, the WGN superstation and radio stations in Denver and Chicago. Operates additional non-owned TV stations under management contracts. Tribune Entertainment develops and distributes first-run programming.
- Cable: Ownership of CLTV in Chicago; 50% of Central Florida News 13; 31% of the TV Food Network. Participates in the regional Fox Sports Channel in Chicago.
- Newspaper publishing: Dailies in Chicago; Orlando, Fla.; Fort Lauderdale, Fla., and Newport News-Hampton, Va.
- Tribune Media services: Entertainment listings and syndicated information for print and electronic media.
- Education: Publishes trade, children's and nonfiction consumer titles and is a major supplier of supplemental educational materials for schools, a unit now up for sale.
- Interactive Media: Manages Web sites and interactive activities for all units, including classified advertising and national services such as auctions, BlackVoices.com, BrassRing.com, cubs.com and Go2orlando.com, a travel planning site.
- Joint ventures: Has equity investments in more than two dozen Internet and high-tech companies.
- Baseball: Chicago Cubs.

The Times Mirror Co.
History

Three businessmen bought the *Los Angeles Daily Times,* printed by the Mirror Printing Office and Book Bindery, in 1882, one year after its founding. Soon joined by Colonel Harrison Gray Otis, who became the *Times'* president, manager and editor in chief, the company was incorporated in 1884. Harry Chandler, who married Otis' daughter, took over the reins as publisher when Otis died in 1917. The company went public in 1938, with the Chandler family retaining control and managing the business through 1986. (The Chandler Trusts controlled 72.6% of the stock.) The company grew and diversified into cable operations, professional information, and book and consumer-magazine publishing.

The family hired Mark H. Willes, an academic and consumer marketer, as CEO in 1995 to improve the company's financial performance and stock price. He did so, but at a price. Under his direction, Times Mirror sold some of the most visible and interesting, but least profitable, operations — including cable systems and the book and directory publishers.

NET REVENUE / OPERATING INCOME (in millions)

	Full year 1998A	Full year 1999E	Full year 2000E
Net Revenue			
Newspaper estimate	$2,308	$2,496	$2,625
Professional Information estimate	212	234	253
Magazine estimate	263	282	296
Corporate & other intersegment eliminations	1	1	0
Total	**$2,784**	**$3,013**	**$3,174**
% growth	16%	8%	5%
Operating Income by unit			
Newspapers	$297	$473	$493
Professional	44	73	71
Magazine	(14)	12	9
Other	95	(75)	(58)
Total operating income before restructuring	**$422**	**$483**	**$515**
% margin	15%	18%	18%

Source: Company reports and PaineWebber estimates.

Attempts to make the *Los Angeles Times'* operations more market-friendly have produced controversy about its integrity. In the top-level reorganization, most of the business executives resigned. Willes shrank news space and laid off 700 people at the *Times* alone, but the stock price soared. As he sought to tear down the "walls" separating the editorial and business sides, journalists charged inappropriate business-side influence on the news. An editorial realignment followed the 1999 publishing of a sports supplement in which the *Times* shared ad revenue with owners of the Staples Center arena (the subject of the supplement) but failed to inform the public. Of late, the *Times* has become a lightning rod for controversy over corporate control of the news.

By the Numbers
- Publishes five metro and two suburban daily newspapers.
- Has won 60 Pulitzer prizes.
- The *Los Angeles Times:*
  - Sells 1.1 million newspapers daily, 1.4 million on Sunday.
  - Represents 40% of Times Mirror profits.
  - Gained 100,000 in new sales from distribution partnerships with ethnic newspapers.
- Publishes 20 special-interest leisure magazines, including *Popular Science, Field & Stream* and *Ski.*

Strategy
From the '60s to the '90s, Times Mirror diversified in numerous ways, only to contract its holdings since 1995. It went in and out of broadcast television, cable, lumber mills, and book and directory publishing in favor of three core businesses: newspapers, consumer magazines and professional information services. Its dailies in Baltimore; Hartford, Conn.; and Long Island, N.Y. (*Newsday*) are dominant, growing and profitable — set to continue as strong local media franchises for publishing and Web-based information services.

The *Los Angeles Times* is the fourth-largest U.S. daily, with the largest local circulation. While other big dailies of comparable strength have "gone national," *Times* executives have chosen to bore more deeply into the Los Angeles basin, with a complex set of relationships supporting business growth. Efforts to grow in San Diego and Orange counties have been unsuccessful. Its *Our Times* local sections serve neighborhoods of about 10,000 apiece. Its partnerships with local ethnic dailies and weeklies yielded circulation increases in 1999. Its Web site is popular, but its growth is not tied to e-commerce.

Business Mix
- Newspaper publishing: seven dailies and a 50% stake in *La Opinión,* Southern California's major Spanish-language newspaper.
- The Los Angeles Times Syndicate and 50% ownership of the Los Angeles Times-Washington Post News Service.
- Twenty consumer magazines, almost all in the sports and leisure category.
- Professional information services in the fields of health and medicine, aeronautics and technology.

···

MARK H. WILLES
Former CEO, The Times Mirror Co.

On his mandate: "I honestly did not have an agenda when I got here except that the company was declining financially. The point of view is that it needed to be fixed. I streamlined the portfolio. Then, I tried to change the cost structure of the units that were left. It was designed to stop the bleeding and get healthy again. If we were going to be healthy again and find a real solution, we needed a change in the fundamental way we grew the business."

The Washington Post Co.

History

The Washington Post, founded in 1877, was acquired for $825,000 by financier Eugene Meyer at a 1933 bankruptcy auction. Meyer "sold" the paper in 1948 to his daughter and son-in law, Katharine and Philip L. Graham, who built up the *Post* from fifth in a five-newspaper market to the dominant D.C.-area newspaper. In 1961, the company added *Newsweek* magazine to its growing holdings. Mrs. Graham gained full ownership after her husband's death in 1962, becoming chairman and CEO in 1973. The Post Co. went public in 1971, with the family maintaining controlling shares. The Grahams' son, Donald, is now publisher, chairman and CEO.

The *Post* built its reputation for courageous coverage when it exposed the Watergate scandal and fought the Nixon administration over threatened denial of broadcast-license renewals in retaliation for publishing the Pentagon Papers.

NET REVENUE/OPERATING INCOME (in millions)

		Full year 1998A	Full year 1999E	Full year 2000E
Net Revenue				
Newspaper publishing		$847	$858	$887
Television broadcasting		358	341	360
Magazine publishing		399	378	395
Cable television systems		298	335	361
Education & other		208	271	350
Total		**$2,110**	**$2,183**	**$2,353**
	% growth	8%	3%	8%
Operating Income		**$379**	**$386**	**$433**
	% margin	18%	18%	18%

Source: Company reports and PaineWebber estimates.
PaineWebber report figures are rounded.

By the Numbers

- Publishes two daily newspapers and more than 40 weeklies.
- The *Post* penetrates 50% of D.C.-area households daily and 70% on Sunday.
- Owns six TV stations, reaching 7.2% of U.S. households.
- Reaches 740,000 cable subscribers in 18 states with the ninth-largest U.S. cable operating system, Cable One.
- Operates 140 educational tutoring centers through its Kaplan subsidiary.
- Processes about 100,000 résumés for about 100 companies monthly via the BrassRing.com employment Web site.

Strategy

The Washington Post Co. has a diverse mix of media properties and a value-driven approach to public ownership. Its small number of shares outstanding trade at prices four or five times the average for media stocks, encouraging institutional rather than individual investment. The company refuses to promise or deliver quarterly growth but does promise increased value. Recent earnings have been flat. The company just lost its COO of 18 years, Alan G. Spoon. Warren Buffett is a major shareholder and board member.

The *Post* and *Newsweek* are central to growing a multimedia national brand. The Post Co. signed an agreement with MSNBC for exclusive commentary on cable programs, for appearances on the NBC network and for *Newsweek's* presence on MSNBC.com. In 1993, the company created its Digital Ink subsidiary, now called Washingtonpost.Newsweek Interactive, to develop the company's editorial and business sites on the Web. It has been upgrading its cable systems to provide high-speed broadband Web access, bypassing cable modem connections and revenue-sharing with cable Internet providers. It has focused on non-urban markets, with broadcasting its most profitable business.

The Post Co.'s Kaplan Educational Centers, known best for college test preparation, have moved into primary school tutoring, college training, professional training and Kaplan University, whose distance-learning programs include the Concord University School of Law, the

DONALD E. GRAHAM
Chairman and CEO, The Washington Post Co.
Publisher, The Washington Post

On the legacy/future: "I worry only about one thing: Do we have the right people everywhere in this organization? Do they have what they need to do their jobs? If The *Washington Post* makes a successful transition into digital technology, it won't have anything to do with me."

nation's first online law school. The Post Co. is majority owner in a joint venture, BrassRing.com, an Internet-based hiring and recruitment management service. It also has acquired several leading computer publications and trade shows, forming its Post-Newsweek Business Information unit.

Business Mix

- Newspapers: *The Washington Post; The Herald* in Everett, Wash.; and two community newspaper groups.
- The Washington Post Writers Group (syndicate) and 50% interest in the Los Angeles Times-Washington Post News Service.
- The *International Herald Tribune,* owned 50% by the Post Co. and 50% by The New York Times Co.
- *Newsweek* magazine; *Newsweek's* international and foreign-language editions; *ITOGI,* a Russian-language newsweekly; and partial ownership of *Tempo,* a Greek-language newsweekly.
- Six TV stations (ABC, NBC and CBS affiliates), Newsweek Productions and a 20% stake in ACTV Inc., providing interactive entertainment and education programming.
- Cable One, a cable-operating system based in Phoenix.
- Kaplan Educational Centers.
- Washingtonpost.Newsweek Interactive, the company's new-media unit.
- Post-Newsweek Business Information services.

Glossary

BROADBAND The term generally used to denote high-speed transmission of large volumes of digital text, photos, audio and video over cable modems, via enhanced telephone lines or by satellite. More literally, broadband is a type of data transmission in which a single wire or signal can carry several channels simultaneously. Cable television uses broadband transmission.

CLUSTERING Amassing multiple media companies in a discrete geographic area to concentrate distribution and deepen market penetration. Newspapers and cable operators are frequent practitioners.

COMMON CARRIAGE An electronic distribution system in which the content is separated from the conduit. Access to the conduit is available to anyone for a fee. Common carriers are usually regulated utilities. Telephone companies are common carriers; anyone can use them to communicate by voice or data stream. Cable operators are not common carriers because they have discretion over their systems' programming and can reject would-be content providers. Congress and federal regulators are reviewing rules governing common carriage, following recent mergers among cable and telephone companies as well as the proposed merger between America Online, the largest Internet content provider, and Time Warner, the second-largest cable operator in the United States. At issue is open access to high-speed Internet connections, especially via cable modems.

CONSOLIDATION The merger of companies within the same industry to create fewer, larger corporate entities. Consolidation often occurs after periods of intense competition, during which the number of companies selling similar products or services increases, with lower profit margins for all. It also occurs when regulatory rules or technology advances change a competitive market.